"There is, of course, n[...]
yourself than to read [...]
learning to read—and all the more with the most important
book in history and the very words of God himself. Gary Millar
is a gifted guide for this most important of pursuits. Learning
to read the Bible will not only give you answers; it will give you
life—the very kind of life in your soul you've been longing for."

DAVID MATHIS, Senior Teacher and Executive Editor,
desiringGod.org; Author, *Habits of Grace*

"Whether you're a new believer in Christ or a grizzled veteran
of Christianity, this book will not only give you the tools to
understand and apply the remarkable truths found in the Bible
but also inspire you as you encounter the astonishing beauty of
God found in his very words."

JULIUS J. KIM, President, The Gospel Coalition

"I recently provided new believers with study Bibles filled with
notes, maps, quotes, and explanations. Instead of finding it
helpful, they were bewildered. If only I could have given them
a copy of this excellent book. From now on I will definitely
recommend that they read this first."

ALISTAIR BEGG, Bible Teacher, Truth For Life

"If you want to be discipled by the voice of God more than the
voice of this world, this book will help you greatly."

RICHARD CHIN, National Director, AFES (Australian Fellowship
of Evangelical Students)

"A simple, clear and immensely helpful guide to getting off and
running with reading the world's best-selling book of all time!"

DENESH DIVYANATHAN, Senior Pastor, The Crossing Church
Singapore; Chairman, Evangelical Theological College of Asia;
President, Project Timothy, Singapore

"*Read This First* gives readers simple steps to understanding God's word and gets their noses into Scripture by getting them to answer questions from the Bible. It works brilliantly for both mature Christians and those who are new to Christian things."

JANE TOOHER, Lecturer in Ministry and Church History; Director, Priscilla and Aquila Centre, Moore College

"Gary Millar has a knack for taking complicated issues and making them clear. More and more people in our churches and in society are unfamiliar with the Bible. Here we find a wonderfully accessible book on how to interpret and understand the Bible. Behind the simplicity of this book is a deep and profound wisdom. An ideal resource for personal study, for small groups, and for continuing Christian education."

THOMAS R. SCHREINER, James Buchanan Harrison Professor of New Testament Interpretation and Associate Dean, The Southern Baptist Theological Seminary

"What could be more important than learning how to read, understand, and apply God's word? *Read This First* is an accessible, encouraging, and jam-packed primer to help you read the Bible. This book answers so many questions—even questions you didn't know you had!"

GLORIA FURMAN, Co-editor, *Word-Filled Women's Ministry* and *Joyfully Spreading the Word*

"This is a wonderful book—fresh, engaging, accessible, practical and rooted in good scholarship. I particularly appreciate the superbly clear examples from Bible passages, and the way Gary Millar makes some pretty meaty thinking come across as not nearly so difficult after all. Thank you so much, Gary! I shall be recommending this with enthusiasm."

CHRISTOPHER ASH, Writer-in-Residence, Tyndale House, Cambridge; former Director, The Cornhill Training Course

READ
THIS FIRST

A Simple Guide to Getting
the Most from the Bible

GARY MILLAR

Read This First
© Gary Millar, 2022. Reprinted 2022.

Published by:
The Good Book Company

thegoodbook.com | thegoodbook.co.uk
thegoodbook.com.au | thegoodbook.co.nz | thegoodbook.co.in

ISBN: 9781784986834 | Printed in the UK

Design by Drew McCall

CONTENTS

Introduction   7

1. Why bother with the Bible?   11

2. Learning to read   25

3. What's the vibe?   39

4. You know what I mean?   53

5. King Context   71

6. It's not about me (although it is!)   87

7. Over to you   101

Appendix: What is the Bible?   115

Recommended resources   125

*For everyone at Elmwood Presbyterian Church, Lisburn,
and especially Sharon, John, Alistair, Pauline and
Mr. Lockhart, who taught me to read the Bible.*

INTRODUCTION

The Millars are definitely a "dog" family. For years, we have had a labradoodle. Our first labradoodle, Hamish, was a shambolic, mischievous bundle of shagginess. The fact that he had three legs for most of his life (after a road accident) somehow just made him even more loveable. But, I have to confess, he was very badly behaved. And it was our fault. We made a cursory attempt to train him with a short spell at "puppy school", but, to be honest, our plans petered out pretty quickly. We didn't really know what we were doing and were easily defeated by his stubbornness—and that combination led, inevitably, to a badly behaved dog.

After Hamish died, we welcomed a new puppy to our family: Nessie (my wife is Scottish!). But this time, we were determined to do a better job with the training. This time, we sought out the help we needed at the beginning. This time, we decided to invest hours, energy and some of our cash into training Nessie. It's been a revelation! We're less than a year in, so there is still a long way to go.

But it is fair to say that something that initially appeared completely baffling to us has, with a little bit of help, become so much clearer. It's still hard work continuing Nessie's training. But thanks to some people who know what they are doing, we're at least on a better trajectory this time around! And owning a dog is a lot less stressful and a lot more enjoyable as a result.

This book aims to help people who would like to read the Bible but don't really know where to start or how to go about it. You may be a Christian who enjoys being part of a church or a Bible-study group, but you end up feeling lost and confused whenever you attempt to read the Bible for yourself. You may have even tried to embark on a Bible-reading regime, but—like me with Hamish—it didn't take long before you gave up with a sense of defeat: you just don't get it. If that's you, don't despair. Lots of us struggle to read the Bible. But that doesn't mean you can't learn how. That's why I've written this book: to guide you through it. My hope is that you'll *read this first* and go back to the Bible with the skills and confidence to truly enjoy it.

Or you may be pretty new to Christianity. You may have always thought that the Bible seems interesting enough for you to take a look, but you've been put off by the small print, strange "religious" language, its distance from your culture, or even just its size. You may have been encouraged to read the Bible by a friend, or heard a snippet of what it says at a wedding or funeral, or come across a quotation somewhere. It's often said that the Bible is one of the best-selling books of all time. That alone seems like a good reason to at least dip into it.

Whatever has brought you to this point, I'd love to help you to get started with reading the Bible. I want to reassure you that reading the Bible is not as baffling as it might initially appear, and that anyone who comes to it with an open mind and a sincere heart can learn to understand and enjoy it—including you.

Read This First assumes nothing. I've tried really hard to "start at the very beginning", and walk through the basics of reading the Bible. If you're completely new to all this, you might want to start with the appendix on page 115 ("What exactly is the Bible?") before jumping into chapter 1.

My aim is to get you (very quickly!) to the point where you can read the words on the page and pick up what they're talking about. Learning to read the Bible—like training a dog—does take a little bit of time and energy. But the payoff is even better: when you read the Bible, you hear the very words of God himself, the Creator of all time and space, speaking to you, personally. And that makes it more than worth the effort.

So, let's get started...

1. WHY BOTHER WITH THE BIBLE?

"All Scripture is God-breathed and is useful for teaching, rebuking, correcting and training in righteousness, so that the servant of God may be thoroughly equipped for every good work."
(2 Timothy 3 v 16-17)

Here are seven good reasons *not* to read the Bible:

1. It is extremely old. (What can it possibly say about life today?)

2. It is hard to read. (As in, hard to understand—although the small print doesn't help either!)

3. It says objectionable things. (About sexuality and slavery, for example.)

4. It describes horrible events. (Like God sending a flood to judge people and whole nations being destroyed.)

5. It has been used to justify terrible things. (Like Apartheid in South Africa, and the Crusades in the Middle Ages.)

6. Life's too short. (Reading it doesn't seem to promise much payback.)

7. Add your own reason here... (Why don't *you* read the Bible?)

Given all that, I wouldn't be at all surprised if you have never read the Bible and don't have much clue about what's in it or why it matters. It seems strange and hard to read. You're wondering, "Why bother?"

ONE COMPELLING REASON TO READ THE BIBLE

I know lots of people who haven't read the Bible for some or all of the reasons above. And I think that's a real shame. For one thing, most of those reasons don't actually stand up.

Yes, the Bible is old, but if we are going to ignore everything that's old on principle, it will make for a deeply impoverished experience of life. Yes, *parts* of the Bible can be hard to understand, but most of it is surprisingly simple (as I hope you'll see by the end of this book). It *does* say some things which challenge all of our values, but since when was that a reason not to read something? And while some parts of the Bible (and the events it describes) are pretty shocking, that's because it is dealing with the real brokenness of our world. In this sense, the Bible is no more shocking than our newsfeed. And even though the Bible's teaching has been abused and misused over the years, had its *true* message been lived out, the world would be a very, very different place.

Whatever you think of the Bible, you can't deny that it's had a huge influence on Western culture. Our language and literature bear the stamp of the Bible at almost every turn. And it contains the teaching of arguably the single most influential individual who has ever walked on this planet—Jesus of Nazareth.

But none of those are the reason why I think you should make reading the Bible a regular part of your life.

I think you should read the Bible because it's unlike any other book you will ever see or handle; when you read the Bible, you read the words of God.

AN UNUSUAL CLAIM

The idea that the Bible is the words of God might sound weird. In one sense, it should sound weird. How can a book be a message from God?

Towards the end of the 1st century, Paul, one of the early leaders of the movement which came to be called "Christianity", wrote to a young protégé named Timothy. In his letter—which is included in the Bible today—he says this:

> All Scripture is God-breathed and is useful for teaching, rebuking, correcting and training in righteousness. (2 Timothy 3 v 16)

Notice that phrase "God-breathed". Paul (who was writing in Greek) may have made up this expression to capture precisely what he wanted to say. His point? That the Bible, even though obviously written by ordinary human beings (like him), has its origin and authority in God himself. This is God's book, which contains God's words, expressed through the personalities and styles of a whole range of human authors. Or, to use Paul's shorthand, the Bible is "God-breathed".

This statement of Paul's comes pretty near the end of the Bible, but it's a claim that's made repeatedly throughout its pages. The first 75% or so of the Bible tells the story of the Israelites, describing how they started out as one (very dysfunctional) family and grew into a great nation, before eventually being overpowered by others. From the very beginning of Israel's story, God's words were right at the heart of their national existence.

After they had escaped from slavery in Egypt (around 3,500 years ago), their leader Moses said that God had acted...

> ... to teach you that man does not live on bread alone but on every word that comes from the mouth of the LORD. (Deuteronomy 8 v 3)

Over the years, God kept speaking to his people, usually through particular spokespeople, such as prophets and kings. The messages were written down and read and reread as the words of God. (This is what we have in our

Bibles as the Old Testament.) That's why King David, Israel's second monarch, who ruled around 1000 BC, could write these words:

The law of the LORD is perfect,
    refreshing the soul.
The statutes of the LORD are trustworthy,
    making wise the simple.
The precepts of the LORD are right,
    giving joy to the heart.
The commands of the LORD are radiant,
    giving light to the eyes.
The fear of the LORD is pure,
    enduring for ever.
The decrees of the LORD are firm,
    and all of them are righteous.

They are more precious than gold,
    than much pure gold;
they are sweeter than honey,
    than honey from the honeycomb.
By them your servant is warned;
    in keeping them there is great reward.

(Psalm 19 v 7-11)

From the earliest times, God's people knew that God had spoken to them, and when his words were written down by human authors, he continued to speak as they were read. It's no accident that the longest chapter in the Bible, Psalm 119, is all about the fact that we need to listen to and act on God's words to enjoy life with him.

In one of its most memorable phrases, the writer calls God's word "a lamp for [our] feet and a light on [our] path" (Psalm 119 v 105).

When Jesus shows up in the 1st century, one of his central claims is that he picks up where the Old Testament prophets have left off, and that he speaks the words of God. This was obviously controversial with the Israelites of his day. Yet in one incident recorded in John's Gospel, as people began to react against Jesus, his friend Simon Peter refused to walk away, saying:

> Lord, to whom shall we go? You have the words of eternal life. (John 6 v 68)

Paul's statement that the Bible is "God-breathed", then, basically summarises what this book says about itself from beginning to end. Yes, it's an actual human book, written by a huge range of people across a vast swath of time. Their personalities and passions come across on every page. But behind all that stands the God who brought this book together and brings it to life. That's what makes the Bible a book like no other.

This book, then—the one that you're holding with my name on the front—isn't intended to improve your literacy or your knowledge of Bible trivia. I've written this book to help you to meet a person—a living, loving being like no other—through the pages of a book like no other. The God of the universe has set things up so that he relates to ordinary people like you and me in real time.

He made us, he loves us, he knows us inside out, and he speaks to us. And he does that through the Bible. That's why reading the Bible matters so much—because when we read it, we meet the one and only God.

THE BOOK LIKE NO OTHER BOOK

Maybe you're still not convinced. To say that the Bible is God's word is a massive claim. How can we possibly prove a claim like that?

When you think about it, outside the world of maths, "proof" is hard to come by. Even in scientific experiments (and criminal investigations!) we're usually dealing with the weight of evidence rather than undeniable "proof". When I get on a plane, no one can actually "prove" that it will stay up. If the aeronautical engineers are right, it should. If it has been constructed properly, it should. Given the fact that lots of similar planes take off and land every day without incident, it probably will. I have flown hundreds of times before without crashing. So even though I can't prove it will stay up, I get on the plane and don't worry too much!

So what are we to do when it comes to the Bible? Well, the Bible *says* it is God's word. Countless people before us have read it to enormous benefit and, after immersing themselves in it, are convinced that it's God's word. My suggestion is simply that, at this point, you "get on the plane" and read it for yourself, with as much of an open mind as you can muster. I suspect that as you read, it won't take too long before you see why this really is a book like no other.

A UNIQUE BOOK REQUIRES A UNIQUE APPROACH

If the Bible is breathed out by God, that means we may need to adjust our approach a little. In many ways, reading the Bible is like reading any other book (as we'll see in the next chapter). But there are some key differences that we need to take on board right at the start.

1. If the Bible is God-breathed, then it demands our attention

My wife, Fiona, is an English Literature teacher by background, and an avid reader. Because of that, there is an endlessly growing pile of books by my bed (and on my Kindle) which Fiona has recommended. I never get through the pile! In fact, I tend to pick and choose. Some of her recommendations are read and relished. But some just get ignored (if I don't like the look of them). Some are started but cast aside after a few pages (if I don't get into them). And to be honest, it doesn't really matter.

But when it comes to reading the Bible, it is a bit different. If the Bible contains God's words, then we can't just "take it or leave it"! If this is how God speaks to humanity, then this book demands our attention.

And that's not all...

2. If the Bible is God-breathed, then we can trust what it says

Usually when we read a non-fiction book or article, it's important to weigh up whether or not it comes from a reputable source. We might try to identify any bias, ask ourselves if it fits with what we already know to be true, weigh up the arguments and so on.

The Bible is different. Its authority (and trustworthiness) comes from God himself. It gives us God's perspective on our world and on us. There's no need to fact-check it because, if it is God who is speaking, then his words are, by definition, true and reliable (and if we do check the facts, we'll always find that they match up anyway). If and when it clashes with our perspective on reality, it's our perspective that's skewed, not his. God's words are profound, wise, searching and life-giving. We really can trust them.

3. If the Bible is God-breathed, then we need to do what it tells us

If we put those two things together—if the Bible comes to us carrying God's authority (as the Creator and Ruler of the universe) and is utterly trustworthy—then we need to do what it says. This a bit different to just *trusting* the Bible. Over the years I have read and ignored quite a lot of books. Books on how to train my dog; how to organise my desk; how to become an ultra-effective leader; and how to make green juices. I have no reason to doubt that those authors wrote true and helpful things. In this sense, I trust them. I just didn't bother doing anything they said.

When we read other books, not only do we assume that we are free to assess what they say; we also know that it is entirely down to us whether we act on whatever it is they are suggesting. And if we don't follow through? It's no big deal. We have probably never met the author, and he or she certainly has no authority to tell us what to do. But what if God himself is the ultimate author? That changes things—we need to do what he tells us! If the God who knows all things speaks to us, then we would be really foolish to ignore what he says. We need to do what this wise and generous God tells us. It just makes sense.

4. If the Bible is God-breathed, then it's worth investing in

The final difference is really the culmination of the others. If the Bible is God's word, then we need to listen to it, believe it and do what it says—and to do all *that* requires investing time and energy into reading it carefully.

Reading the Bible isn't *just* reading words on a page but listening to one who loves us more than life itself, and who has a very clear agenda for our lives and our world. That's why it makes sense to ask for God's help when we read the Bible—help to understand what it means and how it applies to us.

It's also why we can't easily rush reading the Bible. We need to give it time—preferably regular, uninterrupted, unhurried time. These words are ancient—and because most of us don't read a lot of ancient literature, that in itself will slow us down. But more than that, the Bible is so deeply personal—addressing all kinds of weaknesses and sadness as well as awakening all kinds of joys and resolve—that we need to make sure we have time to think carefully about what it means and what it says to us.

When we start to read the Bible, we face twin challenges. The first is the fact that it's so rich—which means learning to read slowly and carefully, word by word, line by line, so that we can squeeze every rich drop of meaning out of what's on the page. But the second is the fact that the Bible is so long. If we are to get the most out of the Bible, and appreciate the soaring storyline which stretches from Book 1 (Genesis) to Book 66 (Revelation), then we need to move quickly enough to get to the end before we've completely forgotten the beginning! We need to learn to read slowly and to read quickly, and to make time to do both. That's why this book will give you some strategies and tools to help you both to savour the detail *and* gasp at the broad sweep of the storyline as you read the Bible.

ONE STEP AT A TIME

There is an old Chinese proverb which says, "A journey of a thousand miles begins with a single step". Getting to know the Bible, God's unique book, starts with reading it. Yes, it might seem daunting. Yes, getting our heads around it may take some time. But from the very first page, we can be sure of two things. First, that God will speak to us—because he *wants* to speak to us and has "breathed out" this book for us. Second, that when God speaks to us, it will change us. We cannot meet with our beautiful and powerful God without being deeply affected. Spending time with this God—who is more tender, more creative, more forgiving, more powerful and more blazingly pure than we can ever imagine—will have an impact on us. As God speaks to us, he has promised to gently correct, shape, humble, challenge, stretch and thrill us. To make us more like Jesus.

And if *that's* what reading the Bible will do, then I really *do* want to read it. Don't you?

YOUR TURN
Read Psalm 19 v 7-14

Think about the implications of the Bible being God's word listed on pages 18-20. What things does the writer of Psalm 19 say about God's word that get at each of the following?

1. God's word demands our attention.

2. God's word is trustworthy.

3. We need to do what God's word says.

4. God's word is worth investing in.

2. LEARNING TO READ

"And pray for us, too, that God may open a door for our message, so that we may proclaim the mystery of Christ, for which I am in chains. Pray that I may proclaim it clearly, as I should."
(Colossians 4 v 3-4)

Cooking for other people has always freaked me out. Take me beyond the two staples that I regularly served up to my student housemates in the distant past and I start to come out in a cold sweat. And then recently, a change in circumstances meant that I needed to cook actual, healthy, nutritious meals for our family two or three times a week. Panic!

Then I discovered this previously unknown thing called a "recipe". It turns out that if I just do a series of pretty basic tasks in the right order, the result is generally edible— even tasty. In the space of a few short weeks, I began to relax and enjoy cooking. The Michelin star may still be a way off, but the stress has gone, and I can loosen up and get on with it.

If we've grasped that the Bible is really important—because it's how God speaks to us and changes us—that obviously makes reading it a big deal. And that's the point at which we can get a bit freaked. "What if I just don't get it?" "I was never any use at English or history at school—how am I going to make sense of the Bible?" "But I hardly know anything about Christianity, let alone the Bible—won't I just be completely lost?" Or perhaps we can't remember the last time we started a book (let alone finished one), and we know that reading just isn't our thing.

I think that most of us feel at least a bit daunted when we start to read the Bible. But there is one very obvious fact that should be immensely comforting: the Bible was written to be understood by ordinary people like us. It doesn't need insider knowledge or a special code to make sense of it. It's not written for experts or professionals. It's written for people like you and me.

We see that in what Paul writes to the early Christians in Colossae (in modern Turkey).

> And pray for us, too, that God may open a door for our message, so that we may proclaim the mystery of Christ, for which I am in chains. Pray that I may proclaim it clearly, as I should. (Colossians 4 v 3-4)

Paul asks the Colossian Christians to pray that he would make the message about Jesus really clear when he speaks. Clarity was always his goal. Whether he was speaking or writing, Paul was determined to make things easy to understand for regular people. That's why he adds, *"as I should"*. This was a point of principle for Paul, and for all the other writers of the Bible too.

This is why the Bible was written in the language that ordinary people actually wrote and spoke. When God spoke to his people, Israel, in the Old Testament, he did so in a language that they could understand (Hebrew). By the time the New Testament was written, Greek was the "English" of the ancient world. It was the language of trade, education and international diplomacy. When it came to writing, there were two options: "classical" Greek, which was used by highly educated people, and which had complex grammar and sophisticated rules; and "common" Greek, the "dumbed down" version, which was used by everybody else. The New Testament writers all chose the "common" option. That's because they wanted their message to be understood.

And whatever language we speak today, God wants to make himself clear to us. That's the principle behind the events of Pentecost in Acts 2, when—soon after Jesus had died, risen and returned to heaven—the early Christians first received the Holy Spirit and started to speak in different languages. This happened during the harvest festival, for which Jewish people from all over the Mediterranean were gathered in Jerusalem. So when the Christians began speaking in lots of different languages, it resulted in this extraordinary scene:

Now there were staying in Jerusalem God-fearing Jews from every nation under heaven. When they heard this sound, a crowd came together in bewilderment, because each one heard their own language being spoken. Utterly amazed, they asked: "Aren't all these who are speaking Galileans? Then how is it that each of us hears them in our native language? Parthians, Medes and Elamites; residents of Mesopotamia, Judea and Cappadocia, Pontus and Asia, Phrygia and Pamphylia, Egypt and the parts of Libya near Cyrene; visitors from Rome (both Jews and converts to Judaism); Cretans and Arabs—we hear them declaring the wonders of God in our own tongues!" Amazed and perplexed, they asked one another, "What does this mean?" (Acts 2 v 5-12)

What did this mean? It meant that God was in the business of making the message of Jesus clear to people from all over the place, in languages that they could all understand. The God who breathes out the words of the Bible is utterly committed to speaking our language! That means that if we read God's words carefully and think about them, and ask him to help, there is absolutely no reason why we shouldn't be able to work out what he's saying to us. And that is very good news indeed!

KEEPING READING (WHY READING THE BIBLE IS LIKE WATCHING NETFLIX)

I am absolutely convinced that every single person who is reading this book already has the skills necessary to read and understand the Bible. Why am I so sure? Let me give you a one-word answer: Netflix. (Or any other streaming service!)

Watching a movie or box set actually requires a very sophisticated set of skills to make sense of what's going on. And it all starts as we simply *watch and listen carefully*.

As the characters are introduced, we instinctively look out for the hints and cues that the writer gives us to answer a whole pile of questions: When and where is all this happening? Is this person "good" or "bad"? Can they be trusted? Are they up to something? Are they hiding anything? What's their relationship with the other characters? Is something terrible about to happen to this person? (The scary music usually gives that one away!) Is this person central to the plot or a bit-part player? And so it goes on. You probably don't say any of this out loud (although some members of my family do!). Nor do you ask all those questions consciously. But it's all going on in your head.

Of course, not all these questions are answered at the start or all at once. If we want to find out the answers, we just have to *keep watching*—at least to the next episode. Sometimes, we have to stick with it for a while to get a sense of what's going on. But we know that if we give it time, everything will start to become clear. It's as we keep watching that we sort out in our heads what's important and what isn't. As the story unfolds, the writer tells us who really matters and who doesn't—who are the main characters and who plays the supporting roles. Gradually, we work out which details are just incidental and which are crucial to the story. And, of course, we do all that instinctively.

The same thing goes for *putting it all together* at the end. At the end of the movie or series, suddenly all the pieces fall into place (or enough of them to come to a satisfactory conclusion, while leaving enough loose ends to justify another season!). We say to ourselves, or to whoever else is in the room, things like "Ahhh—*that's* why he said that to her then. It all makes sense now."

So there really is a lot going on as we watch Netflix—it's just that most of it is instinct.

In a similar way, when it comes to reading the Bible, our greatest need is to read what it says on the page and trust our instincts. God has spoken to us in words, sentences and paragraphs, and we can handle all of those. So we simply read and keep reading, and eventually it will all come together.

JUMP RIGHT IN (WHY READING THE BIBLE IS LIKE WATCHING CRICKET)

If God has already given us all that we need to understand what's going on in the Bible, we just need to jump right in.

"But surely it can't be that simple," you might be thinking. "Don't you have to, like, read a load of books first? Or at least know as much as my friend so-and-so. I don't have a hope of ever becoming a Bible expert like them!"

That's when we need to remember: reading the Bible is like watching cricket.

I am a cricket fanatic. For me, it doesn't get any better than watching a five-day Test match (preferably at the Gabba in Brisbane, where I live, but I don't want to be fussy). Now, lots of people don't get cricket. I don't expect everyone to be able to tell the difference between a "googly" and a "doosra" (that's an off-break bowled with a leg-break action, and a leg-break bowled with an off-break action, if you're interested). But if you came with me and watched 30 minutes of a game, you'd have a good idea of what's going on. One guy hurls a hard ball as quickly (or as sneakily) as possible, and two other guys try to hit it as hard and as far as they can, and when they do, they run up and down. See? What's so complicated about that? You *can* jump right in.

The same is true of the Bible. If we read the words, and then the sentences and paragraphs, and trust our instincts, we can make sense of what's in front of us. Sure, there's a place for "experts". There are all sorts of resources available to us to help us learn more about the history and culture of the time the Bible was written in (and we'll get to those later). And it's important to point out that no one becomes an expert on the Bible overnight. I have been reading, studying and teaching the Bible for most of my adult life, and I've still got so much to learn. *But that doesn't mean that the basic message isn't clear and accessible to anyone.* It is—because, remember,

God is committed to communicating clearly to us. We just need to jump right in.

IS IT REALLY THAT SIMPLE?

Yes, it is! Read the words. If you don't know the words or aren't quite sure of what the writer is getting at, then *keep reading.* As with any good box set, if we keep going, the Bible itself will tell us what's important. Look at the whole sentence and try to make sense of that, and then just keep going, trying to make sense of the whole paragraph, and then just keep going!

How does this actually work in practice? Let's look at a fairly obscure part of the Old Testament first. This is the opening of a book called 1 Kings, which comes in the middle of the story of God's people, Israel.

READ, READ ON, KEEP READING! (EXAMPLE 1)

When King David was very old, he could not keep warm even when they put covers over him. So his attendants said to him, "Let us look for a young virgin to serve the king and take care of him. She can lie beside him so that our lord the king may keep warm." Then they searched throughout Israel for a beautiful young woman and found Abishag, a Shunammite, and brought her to the king. The woman was very beautiful; she took care of the king and waited on him, but the king had no sexual relations with her. (1 Kings 1 v 1-4)

Let's start at the beginning: "When King David was very old, he could not keep warm even when they put covers over him". The sentence isn't complicated. This is about an old man who is feeling cold and can't get warmed up. We may not know who this "David" is, but we know what a king is. It's also pretty clear that this king isn't exactly at the height of his powers. Then his attendants come up with a suggestion: "Let us look for a young virgin to serve the king and take care of him. She can lie beside him so that our lord the king may keep warm." You don't need to have a lifetime of Bible reading behind you to work out that this is a strange—and rather seedy—idea. A young woman will be brought in to keep the king warm. This all seems very odd.

Notice that, so far, you don't need to know anything about who this king is, or his history, or even the particular cultural context where this is taking place (Jerusalem in the 8th century BC) to get the fact that all is not well in this royal palace. And that brings us to an important point: narrative parts of the Bible like this are describing the actions of flawed people in a sinful world—they're not to be interpreted as commands from God, or even as good examples. This one certainly isn't!

If we read on, it just gets stranger and stranger. The search for an appropriate young woman is successful: "Then they searched throughout Israel for a beautiful young woman and found Abishag, a Shunammite, and brought her to the king. The woman was very beautiful." It doesn't take much to work out that the writer wants us to know that this woman climbing into bed with the king was *very beautiful*. And then just in case we missed the point, he spells it out for us at the end of our extract: "She took care of the king and waited on him, but the king had no sexual relations with her." This king, whoever he is, is clearly past his best. Rather than ruling, he's just lying in bed, apparently oblivious to the gorgeous woman beside him.

So what's the point of all that? This man may be the king, but it doesn't look like he's in control. Whatever he was like in the past, now he's a pale shadow of a man who looks like he's on the way down. He's not really much of a king at all. Do you see that? If you do, then you've got the point. This is a picture of an old king who has lost the plot.

Of course, there's more that we could say. If we had time to read the two books before 1 Kings (1 and 2 Samuel), we'd know that this King David is the one who killed Goliath—a red-blooded warrior who had also committed adultery with a beautiful woman called Bathsheba (and orchestrated the death of her husband). That makes his weakness (and sexual disinterest) here all the more striking. But you don't need to know that to get what the text is saying. It also helps to know that God had promised David that one of his sons would rule on his throne after him, so the fact that David couldn't (or wouldn't) get out of bed to declare one of his sons king looks pretty bad. And if we read on in 1 Kings 1, we discover that one of his sons was already outside the palace drumming up support for a coup. But some of that is "googly" or "doosra" stuff—information that it takes time to pick up. And eventually, we'll also want to ask the question, "What has all this got to do with us?" We'll get to that in chapter 6 of this book. But the main things? They are plain and simple. And it's no different when it comes to reading the New Testament.

READ, READ ON, KEEP READING! (EXAMPLE 2)

> Jesus went out and saw a tax collector by the name of Levi sitting at his tax booth. "Follow me," Jesus said to him, and Levi got up, left everything and followed him. Then Levi held a great banquet for Jesus at his house, and a large crowd of tax collectors and others were eating with them. But the Pharisees and the teachers of the law who belonged to their sect complained to his disciples, "Why do you eat and drink with tax collectors and sinners?" Jesus answered them, "It is not the healthy who need a doctor, but those who are ill. I have not come to call the righteous, but sinners to repentance."
>
> (Luke 5 v 27-32)

The first sentence of this extract gives us a whole pile of information. Jesus was out and about and met a guy called Levi, who was a "tax collector" and was "sitting in his booth". For most of us, that probably seems a bit odd. Revenue officials today don't usually sit in "booths" to collect money in person—they just send emails and write letters! So there are clearly some cultural differences here, but just by reading carefully, we can still get to the heart of what's going on.

We're told that Jesus said two words to this tax collector—"Follow me"—and he got up from his booth and went with Jesus. If you think that sounds a bit abrupt, you'd be right. To get up from your desk and walk out of work just because someone tells you to come is a big deal! There is clearly something remarkable going on here between Jesus and Levi. That's confirmed by what happens next, as Levi holds "a great banquet" for Jesus at his house. Whatever Jesus has done for Levi, the tax collector thinks it's pretty special and throws a party. Who's at the party? Lots of other tax collectors.

A party of tax collectors might not sound like our idea of fun. But as we read on, we see it a provoked a strong reaction from some people called "Pharisees" and "teachers of the law" (who sound like academics). They complained to Jesus' followers about him sharing this feast with "tax collectors and sinners". The fact that "Pharisee" gets a capital "P" is a clue that these people weren't *just* narrow-minded busybodies—they were clearly an organised group, or, to use the word in the text, a religious "sect". And it's pretty obvious that they didn't like the crowd at the banquet—whatever they meant by "sinners", it wasn't a compliment! These religious people were annoyed that Jesus was hanging out with the wrong crowd—people who didn't seem to be very religious.

The best way of making sure that we're on the right track is to keep reading. What Jesus says next should help: "It is not the healthy who need a doctor, but those who are ill". Apparently, he didn't come for religious people like the Pharisees (who seemed to think they were healthy) but for the other crowd. Then Jesus says it again in different words, just in case they didn't get it: "I have not come to call the righteous, but sinners to repentance". Jesus says he didn't come for "good" people but for "sinners". That's a surprise. And he calls them to "repentance". That's not a word we use much, but we probably know that it has something to do with being sorry. Jesus says he didn't come for people who are good, but for people who are sorry.

CONVINCED? I HOPE SO...

Of course, there's plenty more to say about these parts of the Bible, but I hope you can see that by simply reading, reading on and keeping reading, it's not that difficult to get to the heart of what God is saying. Which shouldn't be a surprise, because God has gone to enormous lengths to speak clearly to people like us. So go on—jump right in!

YOUR TURN o -
Read Luke 7 v 1-10

Walk through the passage like in the examples on pages 32-37.

1. What is going on in this passage? Imagine talking it through to someone else.

2. What questions do you have as you read? Does the passage itself give you some hints?

3. What is the main thing it is communicating?

For more practice, try doing the same thing with **1 Samuel 1 v 1-20**.

3. WHAT'S THE VIBE?

"For the word of God is alive and active. Sharper than any double-edged sword, it penetrates even to dividing soul and spirit, joints and marrow; it judges the thoughts and attitudes of the heart."
(Hebrews 4 v 12)

It's been a long week, and you are lying in front of the TV looking for something suitably undemanding to watch. Remote control in hand, you scroll through channels and streaming services as quickly as your finger will let you. As the pictures and trailers appear on the screen, how long does it take you to make up your mind? My guess is not long. Cooking show? Not tonight. Sport? Definitely not (or perhaps definitely!). Lions roaming across the savannah in search of tasty zebra? Just had dinner. Is this the right movie? Too old? A bit dark? Don't like her?

In an instant, we recognise what's on the screen, compare it with other similar things we've watched, match the mood with our own, and either press play or scroll on and repeat the process. Simple.

When it comes to reading the Bible, working out what's going on can be a lot tougher. This is why we need to learn to pick up the vibe—the tone or feel of a passage. The vibe also gives us an instant sense of what that part of the Bible is *doing*.

In the same way that the wind lashing against the window and the sound of strings playing minor notes tell us that something awful is about to happen in a horror movie, there are all kinds of written hints which give us a feel for what's going on in a particular passage, how to make sense of what it says, and how we're supposed to react. All we need to do is stand back and pick up the vibe!

We can think about the vibe on a number of different levels. Individual sentences will have a particular vibe (as we'll see with some of Jesus' statements). But those lines form part of a bigger chunk of text, which may also have its own, and perhaps different, vibe—in the same way that there are sometimes really funny lines in an otherwise really scary movie scene. And when we put those "scenes" together, they contribute to the overall vibe of the book as a whole.

Picking this up isn't really all that complicated. As we keep seeing, we just need to jump in and start reading the text!

PICKING UP THE VIBE
Let's start with picking up the vibe of a line. Take the following statements of Jesus recorded in the book of Matthew. What's the vibe of each one?

1. "Go away. The girl is not dead but asleep." (Matthew 9 v 24)

2. "Whoever does not take up their cross and follow me is not worthy of me." (Matthew 10 v 38)

3. "Come to me, all you who are weary and burdened, and I will give you rest. Take my yoke upon you and learn from me, for I am gentle and humble in heart, and you will find rest for your souls. For my yoke is easy and my burden is light." (Matthew 11 v 28-30)

We find all these statements within a few pages of one another, but they all have a very different feel and impact.

When Jesus makes the first statement, he is basically at a wake. A crowd of mourners has gathered outside the home of a twelve-year-old girl who's just died. So what Jesus says is completely outrageous—he tells all the mourners to go home! That sounds pretty rude. But that's when it gets *really* crazy—he tells them they are wasting their time *because she's only sleeping*! That's shocking. In fact, it sounds a bit deranged. Imagine how it made her parents feel. (I should tell you that Jesus goes on to raise the girl to life. But for now, notice just how "out there" Jesus' claim is.)

The second statement feels a bit scary. "Taking up our cross" sounds painful and unpleasant. That's because it was! In the Roman world, there was only one reason for carrying your cross: you were about to be tied (or nailed) to it and executed. So this statement is shocking, demanding and scary. It's a call for us to do something that is really hard and costly.

But when we get to the third statement, Jesus sounds quite different again. This isn't scary or demanding—it's inviting and reassuring. Here, in one of the most beautiful passages in the whole Bible, Jesus speaks tenderly to worn-out people. He describes himself as "gentle and humble in heart" and offers us the deepest kind of rest we can ever imagine. And all we have to do is come to him and rely on him.

I reckon most of us would be able to work out the feel of statements like those without too much difficulty. And that's a vital step to working out the meaning of any part of the Bible. We start by asking what the words mean, as we've seen. Then we need to ask, "What are these words trying to do?" Are they trying to shock us into thinking deeply? To motivate us? To encourage or comfort us? To make us laugh at ourselves? When we can answer that question, we've taken a giant step towards understanding (and then living out) what God is saying to us.

KNOWING WHAT WE'RE DEALING WITH

What about picking up the vibe of a section or passage?

Depending on where we are in the Bible, we could be reading any number of different kinds of writing. We could be reading poetry or prose; listening to a sad song or being led step by step through a detailed, logical argument; hearing a story or being urged to do something urgent RIGHT NOW. How can we tell what we're dealing with? That's where the vibe comes in again.

As we read, we'll start to notice the flow of the text and some of the things that make it hang together. So if it's a story, we'll be introduced to characters—and stuff will happen to them! It will almost certainly have a beginning (which introduces a problem), a middle (which explains how things got more complicated) and an ending (how everything turned out). At points the story may be funny, exciting, sobering or fast-moving. The good thing is that most of us instinctively "get" stories, and real-life stories take up a large part of the Bible. (This is what's sometimes called "narrative".)

At other times, it's pretty obvious that what we're reading isn't a story.

It could be a song, for example. Granted, the Bible doesn't have a soundtrack—but there will be hints to tell us we're dealing with lyrics (like an introductory line that says, "And Moses sang this song"!). We might notice that the lines are a bit shorter and the language a bit more colourful and vivid, and the rhythms a bit different. But there's no need to panic. Ancient songs are pretty much like contemporary songs; they're designed to communicate a feeling and get an idea under our skin (which the writer may even underline for us in a chorus).

Reading through the Bible, we'll come across all kinds of writing: letters (both personal and diplomatic); epic poems; speeches and sermons; family trees and even the occasional parable (short, punchy made-up stories that make us stop and think). Sometimes, the Bible writers— like the best writers always do—"mix and match" different styles, or make up new ones, just to keep us on our toes. But whatever part of the Bible we're in, the main thing is that we jump in, read what's in front of us, and try to pick up the vibe!

If that all sounds a bit daunting, be reassured that in virtually all Bibles, the publishers have given us a little bit of help by adding their own paragraph headings. These help us to find our way round what is a very long book, but they also often tell us what kind of writing we're dealing with in any particular passage.

BIG GULPS OR TINY BITES?

In a way, this next point is pretty obvious, but it's worth saying anyway: we shouldn't read every part of the Bible in the same way. Some parts are written to be mulled over and savoured; other parts are written to be raced through in a single sitting. Some parts are completely straightforward; others take time to get our heads around. Some parts are rich and dense, saying many things; other parts take a long time to say one thing! When we pick up the vibe, it helps us to work out whether we can gulp it down or we need to chew 45 times.

Take a look at two passages. Here's the first:

> Ram was the father of Amminadab, and Amminadab
> the father of Nahshon, the leader of the people of
> Judah. Nahshon was the father of Salmon, Salmon
> the father of Boaz, Boaz the father of Obed and
> Obed the father of Jesse. Jesse was the father of
> Eliab his firstborn; the second son was Abinadab,
> the third Shimea, the fourth Nethanel, the fifth
> Raddai, the sixth Ozem and the seventh David.
>
> (1 Chronicles 2 v 10-15)

This first passage is from the opening section of the books of Chronicles—a one-stop-shop history of God's people from creation to the end of the Old Testament period (in the 6th century BC). It's pretty obvious that it's "just" a list of names. You might recognise David (that's King David, the Goliath guy), but apart from that, most of them are pretty obscure—only a few of them appear in the Bible outside this family tree. That already suggests that these words are intended to be read as a rhythmical account of the passing of the generations—and of God's interest in every individual—rather than to be analysed in intricate detail. The fact that they are actually part of a much bigger family tree, which stretches for a whole nine chapters, confirms that.

The repetitive vibe of the family tree (which isn't all that interesting when its someone else's family!) helps us to see that the main point is a grand sweeping one: God is staggeringly faithful, generation after generation. So we don't need to get bogged down in the detail. We can keep reading quickly, allowing the flood of names we've never heard of to make us marvel at God's faithfulness.

The second extract is a bit different. It's from a letter that Paul wrote to the church in Ephesus:

> Praise be to the God and Father of our Lord Jesus Christ, who has blessed us in the heavenly realms with every spiritual blessing in Christ. For he chose us in him before the creation of the world to be holy and blameless in his sight. In love he predestined us for adoption to sonship through Jesus Christ, in accordance with his pleasure and will—to the praise of his glorious grace, which he has freely given us in the One he loves. (Ephesians 1 v 3-6)

If the family tree in Chronicles hit us with a barrage of names we'd never heard of, this passage hits us with a barrage of words and concepts which blow us away! Almost every word in this section is one we need to stop and think about—*praise, blessed, heavenly realms, chose, holy and blameless, predestined, adoption, sonship* would get us started. The writer, Paul, just keeps piling up big ideas one on top of the other, and it seems as if he talks faster and faster as he goes (and he actually keeps going for another eight verses after this).

What's the vibe? I'd say "intense" or "full-on". That's because Paul is trying to take our breath away with just how spectacular what God has done for us in Jesus really is. He's writing to make us gasp. If we've got that, then we've got the basic point. Sure, there is plenty here for us to chew on for days, if not months—but if we get the vibe, then we'll not go far wrong.

THE BIBLE AS A BOOKSHELF

Individual statements have a vibe. Bigger blocks of text have a vibe. And there's one more thing we need to remember: so do whole books.

There are a lot of books in our house—we have bookcases and bookshelves everywhere! I'd love to be able to tell you that our books are all carefully catalogued and arranged in alphabetical order, but that would be a lie. There is some semblance of order—there are a couple of bookcases devoted to hardback fiction, and a shelf of travel books, and one of theology books near my desk. But apart from that, our "library" is gloriously chaotic, and you never quite know what you might find and where you might find it.

Strange as it may sound, the Bible is like a slightly chaotic bookshelf. Of course, there is some order—the Old Testament (or First Testament, or Hebrew Bible) is at the front and the New Testament at the back. Beyond that, one collection of history books (Genesis – 2 Kings) comes first, followed by a later set (Chronicles – Nehemiah). Then it gets messier, as books written by prophets intermingle with laments, love songs, a hymnbook and a couple more history books. The New Testament is a bit easier to negotiate; it starts with four biographies of Jesus, then a sequel (Acts), followed by a collection of Paul's letters, then the book of Hebrews, and more letters (by early Christian leaders including James, Peter and John) before the book of Revelation, which is a combination of a letter, a prophetic book and something called an "apocalypse" (a book which describes reality in symbolic terms). All that may seem a bit daunting at first, but if we keep reading, we'll soon be able to spot straightaway what kind of book we're dealing with, which makes it much easier to pick up the vibe of individual passages.

The good news is that there are really only a few different kinds—or genres—of books on the "shelf" that is the Bible:

- **Narratives:** These are books that tell a real story set in real places involving real people. In the Old Testament, they either tell the story of God's people during a particular time or the story of an individual member of God's people. In the New Testament, the narrative books are either about Jesus or the church. If you're reading these books, as with any good story, expect to be taken through highs and lows, despair and delight, and made to cry and to laugh.

- **Prophetic books:** These books generally provide God's real-time commentary on the events in the life of God's Old Testament people. Depending on the prophet and what was going on in Israel at the time, these books can be thrilling, confronting, intense, questioning or even very blunt. The prophets tend to express themselves in dramatic terms, using lots of metaphor, with a healthy dose of passion.

- **Collections of "laws":** Sizeable parts of some books (like Deuteronomy 12 – 26) are devoted to describing how God tells his people to live. But the word "laws" is a bit misleading. These parts of the Bible aren't just listing restrictions. As well as commanding his people, God persuades, explains and encourages, and he does it so that they might enjoy a beautiful life with him. Keeping that big picture in mind helps us make sense of what's going on with individual laws.

- **Wisdom books:** Rather than offering God's definitive take on specific events, some parts of the Bible reflect on the messy and often contradictory complexities of life. The book of Proverbs is the classic example, but other books like Ecclesiastes and Job have a similar vibe.

- **Poetic books:** Some books of the Bible are made up entirely of carefully composed Hebrew poetry, which is highly rhythmic and packed with images. So when we read these, we're dealing with figurative language rather than simple historical description. The Song of Songs is like that, and so is Lamentations.

- **Letters:** These make up a large part of the New Testament. Generally from an individual, these letters can be written to other individuals (like Paul's letters to Timothy), or to local churches (like 1 and 2 Corinthians) or even to groups of churches in a large area (Peter's letters). The letters urge the recipients to live out the gospel of Jesus. Some are more positive—others more hard-hitting.

The more you read the Bible, the more easily you'll recognise what kind of book you're reading, and start to notice any similarities between books. But you'll also begin to pick up the hints and nuances that give every book a slightly different tone and vibe. This is one of the things that makes reading the Bible so interesting. It also makes us more sensitive to those sections which stand out from the rest of the book they are part of; sometimes, one part of a book will have a very different vibe to the parts around it. (For example, a warm and loving letter may also raise a very sensitive issue, or a generally upbeat story may have a dark conclusion.) A change in vibe makes us sit up and listen.

GETTING UNDER OUR SKIN

The fact that the Bible is written with such a variety of vibes means that it is the most exciting book in the world. It's written like this so that it will surprise us, comfort us, blindside us, warn us and shock us, as well as instruct us and inform us. It's written to get under our skin.

Sometimes, we can slip into reading the Bible as if it's not much more than a book of obscure trivia—full of information, most of it pretty irrelevant. But God has breathed this book into existence *to change us through it*. He's designed the Bible so that, in the power of the Holy Spirit, it *does things to us*. Of course, sometimes God wants to explain truth to us. But he does so much more than that too. He exposes our basic issues. He highlights our mixed motives. He makes us weep at our failures. He shows us the overpowering beauty of his tender love. He strengthens us by showing us just how strong he is: by revealing the full scope of what he's done for us in the Lord Jesus Christ. He makes us panic and gasp and take stock and say sorry and even collapse into his arms. The Bible is designed to do all that and more.

One Bible writer put it like this: "The word of God is alive and active. Sharper than any double-edged sword, it penetrates even to dividing soul and spirit, joints and marrow; it judges the thoughts and attitudes of the heart" (Hebrews 4 v 12). How does someone get into the deepest recesses of our thinking, decision-making and emotions ("soul and spirit, joints and marrow")? It's not easy. Most of us are fairly self-protective—as well as often being pretty slow on the uptake, if we're honest. That's why God has given us this book in all its variety, quirkiness and richness. And as we read it, he will change us—whether we're ready for that or not!

YOUR TURN

Look at one or more of the Bible passages below and think about the following questions.

1. What's the vibe? (Does it change through the passage?)

2. What type (or genre) of writing do you think this is? (See pages 48-50 for more help.)

3. How does this passage's vibe help to get the message across and under our skin?

Galatians 1 v 1-10

Psalm 150

Amos 5 v 1-15

John 20 v 11-18

4. YOU KNOW WHAT I MEAN?

"I too decided to write an orderly account for you, most excellent Theophilus, so that you may know the certainty of the things you have been taught."
(Luke 1 v 3-4)

Imagine you're sitting in a Bible study, and someone shares what they think a particular verse means. It sounds pretty sensible to you.

But then the person next to you pipes up. They have a very different—and contradictory—opinion. Their take sounds pretty persuasive too.

So now you're not too sure what to believe—especially when the first person comes back with the line, "Well, that's just your interpretation". In other words, *You can't say that I'm wrong.* The awkward silence says it all.

That's because if someone plays the "That's only your interpretation" card, there's not much more to say, unless we want a full-blown argument. After all, who's to say that one person's interpretation is right and the other person's is wrong? Don't we all have the right to our opinions? Isn't it coercive to say otherwise? The only option appears to be staying quiet and going home very confused.

Working out what the Bible means isn't a perfectly exact science. Occasionally there are grey areas which "leave room for interpretation", as we say. But that doesn't mean that every interpretation is equally valid. In fact, there are some interpretations which are right and some which are plain wrong. So how do we tell which is which? That's where the author's intention comes in.

WHY WE DON'T GET TO MAKE UP THE MEANING

I live on a busy road just seven or eight minutes from the heart of the city of Brisbane. Imagine that tomorrow morning, rather than driving to work in the conventional manner (which in Australia means driving on the left), I decide I want a slightly different perspective on my route and drive on the other side of the road instead. After narrowly avoiding head-on collisions with several cars (and their irate drivers), I am pulled over by the police. I explain to the officer that left and right are open to interpretation, and that from now on, I am going to interpret the "left-hand side" as the one closest to my house driving into the city (that is, the side formerly known as right).

What do you think he or she might say? My guess is that their response would colourfully suggest that my interpretation is WRONG!

In the Queensland Highway Code, the Traffic Department of the Government of Queensland has decided that every single occurrence of the word "left" means... well, "left". Neither I nor anyone else is at liberty to interpret it any differently. I can't decide to interpret occurrences on the odd-numbered pages to mean left, and those on the even-numbered pages to mean right. That would lead to confusion and carnage, and probably a jail sentence for me. It would also be unbelievably stupid! It would be to deliberately ignore and distort the intention of the document and the clearly expressed purpose of the author.

Just as the Highway Code was written by someone with a specific purpose, so too the Bible. The ultimate author of the Bible is God himself, and he used particular people (the human writers) at particular moments in history to say something specific—first to the original hearers or readers and then to us.

So when we read the Bible, what matters is understanding what God (the ultimate author) is saying to us through the writer (the human author).

The question is: how do we work out what that is?

The good news is that most of the time, this isn't really all that difficult. Let's look at an example.

LOOKING AT LUKE

Luke wasn't from Israel, and hadn't been around to see Jesus' life and work "in the flesh". He heard the message of Jesus' death and resurrection later. At some point, Luke wrote an account of who Jesus was and what he did (which now features in our Bibles as the Gospel of Luke). He starts by explaining why he is writing:

> Many have undertaken to draw up an account of the things that have been fulfilled among us, just as they were handed down to us by those who from the first were eye witnesses and servants of the word. With this in mind, since I myself have carefully investigated everything from the beginning, I too decided to write an orderly account for you, most excellent Theophilus, so that you may know the certainty of the things you have been taught.
>
> (Luke 1 v 1-4)

Theophilus was a new Christian from a similar background to Luke, and he seems to have commissioned Luke to write his book. So Luke explains that he "carefully investigated everything from the beginning", talking to those who were there, and has written it all down for Theophilus' benefit—in particular, so that Theophilus may "know the certainty of the things" he has been taught. In other words, this book is written to strengthen and encourage faith in the Lord Jesus. Simple!

Because Luke has told us exactly what he's aiming to do, it would be crazy to ignore it. If someone told us they were using Luke's Gospel as a weight-loss programme or as a manual to fix their washing machine, we'd understandably be a bit puzzled. But it's not really any better to read this part of the Bible looking for advice on how to be a good person or how to treat other people better. Luke's book *is designed to teach us about Jesus and help us put our confidence in him*. We mustn't try to take out what the author didn't put in!

BELIEVING IMPOSSIBLE THINGS BEFORE (OR AFTER) BREAKFAST

In Lewis Carroll's fantasy book *Through the Looking-Glass*, the Queen of Hearts tells Alice (of *Wonderland* fame) that she once managed to believe six impossible things before breakfast. Reading the Bible really isn't supposed to be like that! If a particular interpretation is impossible, don't believe it.

To give a trivial example, there is a statement in Genesis 41 v 46 which says that "when he was thirty years old, Joseph began to serve in the court of Pharaoh" (New Living Translation). It would be possible to argue that Joseph was employed as the Egyptian ruler's tennis coach—possible but wrong. The writer couldn't possibly mean that! Obviously, tennis hadn't been invented. But more than that, the Hebrew words used have very specific meanings that are tied up with being employed at the royal palace: "serve" means "work for", and "court" means "household" or "service". Any connection between the English translations of the Hebrew words and the game of tennis is purely accidental! The "tennis" interpretation is simply impossible.

Or, more seriously, look at these words written by the apostle John: "No one who continues to sin has either seen [Christ] or known him" (1 John 3 v 6). At first glance, that's quite worrying! I, for one, do continue to sin (in what I think, say and do), and John seems to be saying that means I don't know the first thing about Christ and certainly don't belong to him.

But it *can't* mean that, for two reasons: (1) it doesn't fit with the rest of the New Testament, which insists that Christ came for messed-up people like us, who continue to get it wrong even after we come to trust in Jesus; and (2) it definitely doesn't fit with what John has already said in his letter. Here's 1 v 8-9: "If we claim to be without sin, we deceive ourselves and the truth is not in us. If we confess our sins, he is faithful and just and will forgive us our sins and purify us from all unrighteousness."

So, John has already said that we all mess up and that to pretend otherwise is delusional. For him, continuing to sin (in 3 v 6) doesn't mean mucking it up sometimes when we're trying to live for Jesus. He's talking about people who refuse to do what God says and make sin a lifestyle choice. John's point is that belonging to Jesus is incompatible with doing exactly what you want all the time.

It is true that there are some pretty remarkable claims made by the Bible (like the fact that Jesus rose from the dead, for example), but, as a general rule, if the interpretation we've come up with seems impossible (because the writer couldn't have said that or because it doesn't fit with one of the Bible's big points), then we've probably got it wrong.

THE MAIN THINGS ARE THE PLAIN THINGS (AND THE PLAIN THINGS ARE THE MAIN THINGS)

One of the great temptations when we are reading the Bible on our own—and one of the great frustrations when we are reading it with other people—is going off on a tangent. Sometimes, all it takes is a bit of word association or a personal memory to send our minds spiralling off into the deep blue yonder—but the particularly challenging kind of tangents are those which start off at least as genuine attempts to work out what's going on in the text.

Now, it's hard to get the balance here. The Bible is such an infinitely rich and textured book that there is delight to be found in every name in the family trees in the books of Chronicles, every embroidered pomegranate in the design for the Tent of Meeting in Leviticus, and every "horn" of every creature in the book of Revelation. But it's also possible to get so bogged down in the details that we miss the *main thing* that the writer wants us to focus on.

An old friend of mine had this mantra: "The main things are the plain things, and the plain things are the main things". In other words, the things the author wants to emphasise are the things he makes obvious; which means that the obvious things are the ones we should focus on.

It's not that the main thing is the *only* thing in any part of the Bible, but it is the main thing! It's not that *every*thing in every part of the Bible is obvious straightaway, but the main things are.

I've tried to allow that to guide my own Bible reading. In fact, I'd say it's the single most helpful principle for reading the Bible I know: the main things are the plain things, and the plain things are the main things.

A couple of examples should help flesh this out.

1. JOSEPH IN POTIPHAR'S HOUSE

The first example comes from the story of Joseph (the one of "Amazing Technicolor Dreamcoat" fame). Joseph's story is epic and stretches over the final 14 chapters of Genesis. We'll pick it up in chapter 39. By this point, Joseph has already been sold into slavery by his jealous brothers, who have had enough of their father's blatant and unwise favouritism. Joseph finds himself in Egypt, in the household of one of Pharaoh's military commanders, by the name of Potiphar.

> [1] Now Joseph had been taken down to Egypt. Potiphar, an Egyptian who was one of Pharaoh's officials, the captain of the guard, bought him from the Ishmaelites who had taken him there. [2] The LORD was with Joseph so that he prospered, and he lived in the house of his Egyptian master. [3] When his master saw that the LORD was with him and that the LORD gave him success in everything he did, [4] Joseph

found favour in his eyes and became his attendant. Potiphar put him in charge of his household, and he entrusted to his care everything he owned. [5] From the time he put him in charge of his household and of all that he owned, the LORD blessed the household of the Egyptian because of Joseph. The blessing of the LORD was on everything Potiphar had, both in the house and in the field. [6] So Potiphar left everything he had in Joseph's care; with Joseph in charge, he did not concern himself with anything except the food he ate.

Now Joseph was well-built and handsome, [7] and after a while his master's wife took notice of Joseph and said, "Come to bed with me!" [8] But he refused. "With me in charge," he told her, "my master does not concern himself with anything in the house; everything he owns he has entrusted to my care. [9] No one is greater in this house than I am. My master has withheld nothing from me except you, because you are his wife. How then could I do such a wicked thing and sin against God?" [10] And though she spoke to Joseph day after day, he refused to go to bed with her or even to be with her.

[11] One day he went into the house to attend to his duties, and none of the household servants was inside. [12] She caught him by his cloak and said, "Come to bed with me!" But he left his cloak in her hand and ran out of the house. [13] When she saw that he had left

his cloak in her hand and had run out of the house, [14] she called her household servants. "Look," she said to them, "this Hebrew has been brought to us to make sport of us! He came in here to sleep with me, but I screamed. [15] When he heard me scream for help, he left his cloak beside me and ran out of the house." [16] She kept his cloak beside her until his master came home. [17] Then she told him this story: "That Hebrew slave you brought us came to me to make sport of me. [18] But as soon as I screamed for help, he left his cloak beside me and ran out of the house."

[19] When his master heard the story his wife told him, saying, "This is how your slave treated me," he burned with anger. [20] Joseph's master took him and put him in prison, the place where the king's prisoners were confined.

But while Joseph was there in the prison, [21] the LORD was with him; he showed him kindness and granted him favour in the eyes of the prison warder. [22] So the warden put Joseph in charge of all those held in the prison, and he was made responsible for all that was done there. [23] The warder paid no attention to anything under Joseph's care, because the LORD was with Joseph and gave him success in whatever he did.

How do you work out what the main point of this narrative is? Here are a few clues:

1. Where does the story begin and end?

It's always good to pay close attention to the beginning and end of the story. In this case, it starts and ends with Joseph and the LORD, who is directing events (see verses 3 and 5 at the start, and verses 21 and 23 at the end).

2. Who are the characters, and where is the focus?

The spotlight remains on Joseph all the way through. We don't find out anything about either Potiphar or his wife, other than the way in which they related to (and mistreated) Joseph. The writer makes no "editorial" comments about their behaviour or even about Joseph's actions—they are not the focus. Events move quickly from one catastrophe to another, but behind the scenes, God remains in control.

3. How does this fit in with the flow of the "big story"?

In this case, it helps to have read to the end of Genesis to find out how Joseph's story ends. According to Genesis 50 v 20, God was using all these events to get Joseph into a position of power in Egypt so that he could keep his family alive during a famine. And when we step back and look at the big story of the Bible, we see why that's important: because God had chosen to work through this family to bring his rescuer, Jesus, into the world generations later. (Jesus was a descendant of one of Joseph's brothers, Judah.) This means that the main point of this story is actually about God rather than Joseph.

By answering these simple questions, hopefully it has become clear that the writer's main focus in Genesis 39 is on the fact that God is in control. He was working to get Joseph in the right place at the right time to save his family (thus keeping God's grand rescue plan on track— but more of that in the next chapter). Is Joseph a good example of sexual morality? Of course. Does he cope well with injustice? It looks like it. But none of these things are the main thing. The main point is very clear at the start and the end: God is in control and is working on something big.

2. THE GOOD SAMARITAN

This second example is perhaps the most famous story that Jesus ever told. It's usually called "The Parable of the Good Samaritan". Read it carefully:

> [25] On one occasion an expert in the law stood up to test Jesus. "Teacher," he asked, "what must I do to inherit eternal life?"
>
> [26] "What is written in the Law?" he replied. "How do you read it?"
>
> [27] He answered, "'Love the Lord your God with all your heart and with all your soul and with all your strength and with all your mind'; and, 'Love your neighbour as yourself.'"
>
> [28] "You have answered correctly," Jesus replied. "Do this and you will live."

[29] But he wanted to justify himself, so he asked Jesus, "And who is my neighbour?"

[30] In reply Jesus said: "A man was going down from Jerusalem to Jericho, when he was attacked by robbers. They stripped him of his clothes, beat him and went away, leaving him half-dead. [31] A priest happened to be going down the same road, and when he saw the man, he passed by on the other side. [32] So too, a Levite, when he came to the place and saw him, passed by on the other side. [33] But a Samaritan, as he travelled, came where the man was; and when he saw him, he took pity on him. [34] He went to him and bandaged his wounds, pouring on oil and wine. Then he put the man on his own donkey, brought him to an inn and took care of him. [35] The next day he took out two denarii and gave them to the innkeeper. 'Look after him,' he said, 'and when I return, I will reimburse you for any extra expense you may have.'

[36] "Which of these three do you think was a neighbour to the man who fell into the hands of robbers?" [37] The expert in the law replied, "The one who had mercy on him."

Jesus told him, "Go and do likewise."

(Luke 10 v 25-37)

The problem with well-known stories is that sometimes we think we know what they mean before we've actually read them. That means it's doubly important to read carefully. As before, these suggestions might help:

1. Where does the story begin and end?

Reread verses 25-29. Jesus is being questioned by a religious expert who is interested in getting "eternal life". But what does Jesus tell him to do (v 27-28)? Does anything strike you as strange about that? Jesus basically tells the man to do the impossible! That should tell us that something unusual is going on here. A quick glance at how the story ends confirms that. What does Jesus tell the man to do at the end (v 37)? Jesus takes the man's question ("Who is my neighbour?") and flips it on its head (*Go be a neighbour*). Why, do you think?

2. Who are the characters and where is the focus?

In the parable itself, the first two characters who walk by are Jewish religious leaders ("good" guys), but the third one is a Samaritan (a kind of renegade Jew from the neighbouring territory, who was definitely regarded as a "bad" guy). What is Jesus' intention in making the bad guy not only the hero of the story but the example for this pretty smug Jewish "expert" to copy?

3. How does this fit in with the flow of the "big story"?

Everywhere else in his public life Jesus tells people to come to him to be saved instead of trying to be good themselves. Given that, what do you think might be going on here? Why does he challenge the man so bluntly at the end?

Even if you don't get all the details, I hope you can see that this isn't really a story about caring for the poor. (At least, that isn't the main thing.) It's a discussion (a very challenging discussion) about *eternal life*. The expert in the law wants to know just how high Jesus thinks the bar is to get into God's good books. Jesus forces him to raise the bar as high as he can imagine—and then to raise it some more! The "main thing" in this story is that if we are relying on what we do to gain God's approval (to get "eternal life"), then we are going to fail. It's just too hard. The implication is that what we really need is someone to come and show us mercy.

DON'T PANIC...

Both of those examples looked at narratives, but similar principles apply when we're reading other types of writing in the Bible too (like letters or poetry).

1. How does the passage begin and end? (Is there an introductory and/or a concluding statement? Is the writer taking us along a chain of ideas?)

2. Where is the writer's focus? (What words are repeated? What points are underlined? Is there an idea that serves as a centrepiece?)

3. How does it fit in with the flow of the "big story"? (More on this in the next chapter.)

If all that feels a bit bewildering, don't panic. In the next couple of chapters, we're going to start putting things together in a way which will go over everything we've covered so far. But for now, just remember that when it comes to interpreting the Bible, it isn't just the loudest voice—or the strongest opinion—that wins. Not all interpretations are equally valid. The Bible means what God meant it to mean. And by paying close attention to what the author intends to communicate, we can avoid confusion and be confident that we are hearing what God wants to say.

YOUR TURN ○ -

The book of Acts tells the story of the Christian movement in the decades after Jesus' death, resurrection and return to heaven. **Read Acts 12 v 1-24** and answer the questions as in the examples on pages 60-67.

1. Where does the story begin and end (v 1-4, v 23-24)?

2. Who are the characters and where is the focus?

3. How does this fit in with the flow of the "big story"? (Read Acts 1 v 8 to see the mission Jesus gave his disciples right at the beginning, and which flows through the rest of the book.)

4. Given your answers to questions 1-3, what do you think is the main thing this passage is about? (What are some of the things that *aren't* the main thing?)

Try doing the same thing with **Exodus 1 v 1-22**. In the previous book, Genesis, God promised Abraham that his family would grow into a great nation with their own land. At the end of Genesis, Abraham's grandson, Jacob, went to live in Egypt with his family.

1. Where does this part of the story begin and end (v 7, v 20)?

2. Who are the characters and where is the focus?

3. How does this fit in with the flow of the "big story" that started in Genesis?

4. Given your answers to questions 1-3, what do you think is the main thing this passage is about? (What are some of the things that *aren't* the main thing?)

5. KING CONTEXT

"These things happened to them as examples and were written down as warnings for us, on whom the culmination of the ages has come."
(1 Corinthians 10 v 11-12)

One of the beautiful things about reading is that it has the power to transport us in our minds to times and places we have never been to. Books take us to *their* world in order to say something to us about *ours*. And that's basically how reading the Bible works.

Dick Lucas, the former Rector of St Helen's Bishopsgate, in the heart of the City of London, always emphasised the importance of getting into the world of the Bible. If he was preaching on Paul's letter to the Corinthians, for example, he would say, "We have to travel to Corinth before we come to London". In other words, if we are going to read the Bible well, then we have to read it *in context*. We need to work out what the words *meant* "back then" before we can work out what they mean for us now. We can't make the words mean something completely different today from the writer's intention in his day. So we need to "pack our bags" and put ourselves in the place of the original writer(s) and reader(s) before we try to work out what the Bible is saying to us.

Hopefully that sounds pretty reasonable. If you want to read Shakespeare, then knowing a bit about Elizabethan England clearly helps. But how much do we need to know in order to get what the Bible is on about? Do we all have to learn Hebrew and Greek? Or become experts in ancient history? Or go to Bible college for three or four years before we can get anything out of the text? These are all good things to do (and, as a principal of a Bible college, I'm all for them!)—but we don't *need* any of these things to understand the Bible. God has spoken clearly to us through the Bible, and the Holy Spirit helps us to understand what he is saying. We must never let go of that. But the simple fact remains that to make sense of any text, we need to pay attention to the context. In the case of the Bible, that works at three levels:

- **The "local" context:** How people lived at the times and in the places where the Bible was written.

- **The "historical" context:** What was going on in the world at the time.

- **The "biblical" context:** How the part we're reading fits into the flow of the whole story of the Bible and shows us Jesus.

The great news is that it's relatively easy to pick up most of this knowledge by reading the Bible itself, and by having just a few good resources to hand. (You'll find some recommendations on pages 125-126.) In the rest of this chapter, I just want to walk you through what this looks like in practice.

To keep things simple, we'll use the Old Testament book of Ruth as our main example. Ruth is short (only four chapters), beautifully written, and has a marvellous ending. So before reading the rest of this chapter, it would be helpful if you put this book down for a few minutes, made yourself a cup of good coffee (or tea if preferred) and read Ruth right through...

LEVEL 1: STAYING LOCAL

I've moved cross-culturally a few times in my life. Northern Ireland to Scotland. Scotland to England. England to Northern Ireland. Northern Ireland to the Republic of Ireland. The Republic of Ireland to Australia. (I'll leave you to guess which caused the biggest culture shock— but it wasn't moving to Australia!) While most of those places are only a few hundred miles apart and my native language is spoken in all of them, there were nonetheless still enough cultural differences for me to embarrass myself. In each place, I've caused much confusion and got many blank looks because I didn't quite get the local "lingo" or context.

So, in the UK and Ireland, "hoover" can be used as a verb. But not, apparently, in Australia. Down under, a cool box isn't a cool box but an "Esky" (short for "Eskimo"). Language isn't the only difference. Not surprisingly, most houses here in Brisbane don't have central heating and are built to catch the breeze and let it in. In the UK, houses are designed to do the opposite: to keep the cold out and the heat in. Double glazing, insulated brick walls and tightly fitting doors are what's needed. I could go on, but you get the picture. Life is just a bit different in every place, and it helps to know that.

Of course, none of this is "specialist" knowledge for insiders. We pick these things up naturally by listening or asking questions. I have a colleague who is hooked on Korean dramas, or "K-dramas". You could almost say he's an expert. But he has only been to Korea once and, to my knowledge at least, hasn't taken a course or read a book on this particular art form! He's just picked it up by watching and listening, and occasionally googling something.

It's this kind of local knowledge that we need to pick up as we read the Bible. But *don't panic*—the more you read the Bible, the more it will start to feel like home.

HOW THIS HELPS US READ RUTH
Ruth is packed full of little details of rural life in early Israel. For example, Ruth suggests in 2 v 2, "Let me go to the fields and pick up the leftover grain behind anyone in whose eyes I find favour". This was a standard practice set up by God in an earlier book of the Bible (Leviticus 19 v 9 and 23 v 22). The harvesting was deliberately inefficient so that grain was left behind for poor people like Ruth to gather.

Lying behind Ruth 3 v 9 is a practice by which unmarried male relatives had the right to marry childless widows, offering them protection, security and a future. But according to the ever-scrupulous Boaz in verses 12-13, it wasn't a matter of first-come, first-served, but operated on a "closest relative has first choice" principle.

When we come to chapter 4, however, we see that this transaction was actually quite complex. It took place "at the city gate", an open area where the town business was transacted, and involved not just marrying the widow but buying the deceased husband's land, preserving his name and securing his inheritance for the future—oh, and swapping sandals to seal the deal.

Appreciating these little local details has the marvellous effect of bringing these events into sharper definition, enabling us to see what happens in more vibrant colours.

BONUS EXAMPLE: THE CHURCH AT LAODICEA

Local context helps us as we read the New Testament too. At the start of the book of Revelation, the apostle John has a vision of Jesus speaking directly to seven churches in the Roman province of Asia Minor (part of Turkey today). To the church of Laodicea he says, "I know your deeds, that you are neither cold nor hot. I wish you were either one or the other! So, because you are lukewarm—neither hot nor cold—I am about to spit you out of my mouth" (Revelation 3 v 15-16). These are pretty strong words, but they are also a bit strange!

For us, especially when it comes to levels of enthusiasm, "hot" is good, "lukewarm" is not so good and "cold" is bad. But Jesus says that "hot" and "cold" are good, but "lukewarm" is bad! That means he probably isn't talking about enthusiasm. Nor does it make much sense if he is saying that he would rather people hate him than feel indifferent about him.

So what is he on about? The clue is actually at the start— he is talking about their "deeds", and the fact that they are pretty useless. That's confirmed by a little bit of local knowledge. Up the road from Laodicea, in Hierapolis, they had hot springs—extremely useful for washing clothes and bathing. Down the road in Colossae, they had really cold water—great for drinking. And in Laodicea? Yes, you guessed it: lukewarm, chalky water, which was rubbish for washing things and horrible to drink. Useless really. The point isn't really about the Laodiceans' enthusiasm at all but about their *usefulness*. We can get there from the text, but a little bit of background makes all the difference.

LEVEL 2: BIG HISTORY

Alongside the advantage of getting to know some of the little stuff which makes up the background of whatever passage we're reading, it's also really important to work out where it fits in the big story of the Bible.

The Bible covers events from the creation of the universe to the establishment of the church in the years following Jesus' death and resurrection. That's quite a sweep! But the major movements of the text can be mapped out in eight simple words:

1. Creation

2. Fall

3. Covenant

4. Kingdom

5. Exile

6. Return

7. Jesus

8. Church

If we can remember those eight words, we can't go too far wrong.

- **Creation:** They don't take up much space, but Genesis 1 and 2 set things up for everything else. God made the world, and it was good.

- **Fall:** Adam and Eve disobey God (Genesis 3), introducing the massive problem that God solves in the rest of the Bible: sin.

- **Covenant:** No sooner have Adam and Eve messed up than God promises to sort things out. (Genesis 3 v 15 is the first hint of this.) He does this by making promises to people. Essentially they all boil down to this: *I will be your God; you* *will be my people*. God calls this promise-based arrangement his "covenant". God works with one family (Abraham's), eventually growing it into a nation (Israel), which he rescues from Egypt (the book of Exodus) and leads into a beautiful new land (the book of Joshua), where he sends "judges" to govern them (the book of Judges).

- **Kingdom:** It isn't long before God's special "covenant" people want to be just like everyone else, and demand a king (1 Samuel). The rest of the books of Samuel and Kings tell us how that worked out. Israel's first three kings—Saul, David and Solomon—get plenty of airtime, before the nation splits in two (1 Kings 12), into a northern kingdom, Israel, and a southern one, Judah. We meet the rest of the kings of Israel and Judah in a fairly depressing procession of ungodliness (1 and 2 Kings), often exposed and highlighted by prophets, who also wrote their messages down in books (e.g. Amos, Hosea, Isaiah). The point? God's people really do need a better king than these.

- **Exile:** By the end of the books of Kings, Israel has been decimated by Assyria (722 BC), and Judah has been mostly carted off into captivity by the Babylonians (586 BC). The books written in the run-up to or during the Babylonian Exile (e.g. Jeremiah, Lamentations, Daniel) have a very different vibe to those written in Israel's heyday.

- **Return:** Eventually, some of the people of Judah make it back home (70+ years later). But things are never quite the same. After the exile, most things are a shadow of what they were: the temple is second-rate, rebuilding the walls of Jerusalem takes an age, and most of the people seem pretty half-hearted (Nehemiah, Ezra and the prophets Haggai and Malachi). The Old Testament finishes with a whimper and a growing awareness that God will have to do something spectacular to change anything.

- **Jesus:** In the four Gospels (Matthew, Mark, Luke, John), God announces that his solution to the disappointment and mess of the Old Testament is Jesus himself. Even though God's people are under Roman occupation and are deeply divided, God in the flesh steps into the middle of it all, to die and rise for people of every nation.

- **Church:** The staggering implications of Jesus' death and resurrection are traced out for us as the gospel message spreads. The lives of the first churches are a glorious mixture of messiness, joy and suffering! (Acts and the letters such as Romans, Philippians, James.) And we look forward to the day when the struggle will be over, and Jesus will return to live with his people in a glorious new creation (Revelation).

HOW THIS HELPS US READ RUTH

The book of Ruth starts like this: "In the days when the judges ruled, there was a famine in the land. So a man from Bethlehem in Judah, together with his wife and two sons, went to live for a while in the country of Moab" (Ruth 1 v 1). The first detail we need to note is that these events took place "in the days when the judges ruled". That's referring to the main characters in the book of Judges, which is the book before Ruth in our English versions. That puts us in the "covenant" phase of the Bible's story line. God had committed himself to his people, but the people...? Well, they weren't so committed. The book of Judges sums up this period with the slogan "All the people did whatever seemed right in their own eyes" (Judges 21 v 25, NLT). When we're told that Elimelek and Naomi's family lived during this period, it's suggesting that we don't assume too much about their devotion to God!

That's backed up by the fact that when there was a famine, they moved to Moab. Moab (part of Jordan today) was not the favourite holiday destination of pious Israelites—Israelites and Moabites really did not get on. The Moabites also worshipped a particularly odious god called Chemosh, whose trademark was demanding child sacrifice. The fact that Elimelek and Naomi went to Moab either means they were utterly desperate or they just didn't care much about God. But then, that's what most people were like in this period. Knowing that isn't completely vital for understanding what's going on, but it really does help—the darkness implied in this opening makes God's grace shine even more brightly as the story develops.

LEVEL 3: IT'S ALL ABOUT JESUS

Not only is the Bible one big story, it also fits together to convey a consistent message: it's all about Jesus. All through the Bible, God is working to bring people like us to know and enjoy him through Jesus, and to delight in him forever in a completely fixed-up universe.

If you need convincing, then try the classic trick of looking at the beginning and the end! If you read Genesis 2 v 4-14 and Revelation 22 v 1-5, you'll see some startling similarities. The story starts in a garden and it ends in one too—one where God himself meets with his people. There is no sin to disrupt our relationships. Instead, we get to know and enjoy God. Everything that happens in between Genesis and Revelation is all about what God does through Jesus to make that possible.

The way that story is told, of course, is both rich and complex. The 66 books of the Bible don't all fit into an unbroken narrative, but they do contribute to a detailed tapestry which depicts what God has done and will do in Christ in vibrant colours. The overarching message of the Bible is like a rope made of many strands. These "strands" or themes run all the way through the Bible. Sometimes they are easy to spot; at other points they disappear, only to return many years (or books!) later. There are around

20 themes which make up the big story of the Bible. Some of them are:

kingdom	covenant
salvation/rescue	sin
sacrifice/atonement	holiness
humanity	people of God
city of God	land
exile	return/reconciliation

If many of those don't make sense to you right now, that's ok. One of the brilliant things about reading the Bible is how you continue to discover new ways in which these themes weave together—even after you've been reading it for years.

All of the themes find their ultimate fulfilment in Jesus. Jesus himself made that obvious when he "bumped into" two of his friends after his resurrection. No doubt to their great embarrassment, they didn't initially recognise who he was (though in their defence, they weren't expecting to meet a resurrected friend that afternoon, and in any case, they probably had their heads and faces covered to protect themselves from the dust). But Jesus spent time showing them how the whole Bible actually points to him:

> And beginning with Moses and all the Prophets, he explained to them what was said in all the Scriptures concerning himself. (Luke 24 v 27)

A few hours later, he met with his closest friends in a room in the city of Jerusalem. And he did exactly the same thing:

Then he opened their minds so they could understand the Scriptures. He told them, "This is what is written: the Messiah will suffer and rise from the dead on the third day, and repentance for the forgiveness of sins will be preached in his name to all nations, beginning at Jerusalem. (Luke 24 v 45-47)

C.H. Spurgeon was a 19th-century preacher in London. He told a story in which a younger preacher was told:

"Don't you know, young man, that from every town, every village and every hamlet in England, wherever it may be, there is a road to London? ... So from every text of scripture there is a road to Christ. And my dear brother, your business is, when you get to a text, to say, 'Now, what is the road to Christ?'" (Sermon number 242)

Wherever we are in the Bible, if we keep reading, we will (sooner or later) be pointed to Jesus by the text itself. It really is all about him.

HOW THIS HELPS US READ RUTH

After Ruth marries Boaz, they have a child named Obed—and everyone, including Grandma Naomi, lives happily ever after. But that's not the point of the story. Here's how it finishes:

> [18] This, then, is the family line of Perez:
>   Perez was the father of Hezron,
> [19] Hezron the father of Ram,
>   Ram the father of Amminadab,

²⁰ Amminadab the father of Nahshon,
  Nahshon the father of Salmon,
²¹ Salmon the father of Boaz,
  Boaz the father of Obed,
²² Obed the father of Jesse,
  and Jesse the father of David. (Ruth 4 v 18-22)

The writer takes us back several generations to Perez, son of Judah, from whom it was promised rulers would come (see Genesis 46 v 12; 49 v 10); and then fast-forwards to Obed, the newborn; but then *keeps going* all the way to King David. Suddenly it becomes clear why this story of seemingly ordinary people is included in the Bible: this is the family tree of King David. And because of that, it's the family tree of Jesus himself! Sure enough, in the genealogy of Jesus in Matthew 1 we find Boaz and Obed, and even Ruth herself (Matthew 1 v 5). The book of Ruth shows us God's loving kindness to his people—and ultimately, his loving kindness to us in sending Jesus.

THE GOSPEL-SHAPE OF THE BIBLE

Context really does matter when we read the Bible. The local context matters. The historical context matters. But most of all, the *biblical* context matters.

When we realise that every part of the Bible is driving us to Jesus, we will make sure that we read every part of the Bible in a way which fits with this overall message. And when we do, we can't help but be blown away, as we worship our saviour Jesus.

YOUR TURN ○ -

Read the following passages and write down anything you notice about the three levels of context. Don't worry if there is more in one category than another:

1. *Local context:* What hints do we get about life at the time this was written? What else might it be helpful to know in order to understand this passage better? Where could you go for answers?

2. *Historical context:* At what point in Bible history does this passage come? (See pages 76-79.) How does that help us to work out what's going on? What light does that shed on this passage?

3. *Biblical context:* How does this passage point you to Jesus? Pause to praise him in prayer.

Genesis 22 v 1-19

1. *Local context:*

2. *Historical context:*

3. *Biblical context:*

1 Peter 1 v 3-9

1. *Local context:*

2. *Historical context:*

3. *Biblical context:*

Psalm 72

1. *Local context:*

2. *Historical context:*

3. *Biblical context:*

6. IT'S NOT ABOUT ME (ALTHOUGH IT IS!)

"All Scripture is God-breathed and is useful for teaching, rebuking, correcting and training in righteousness, so that the servant of God may be thoroughly equipped for every good work."
(2 Timothy 3 v 16-17)

We're almost ready to put everything we've seen so far together. But before we do that, there's a final step that is very important. That's because there are two mistakes it's really easy to make when we read the Bible, and both of them will play havoc with us actually getting what's going on. But with this final step in place, we'll be well on the way to a healthy, sustainable, nourishing pattern of reading this peerless book. We'll be able to hear the living God of the universe speak powerfully into the messy details of our days and change the way we live our Tuesday morning or Saturday afternoon.

MISTAKE #1: ACTING AS IF THE BIBLE HAS NOTHING TO DO WITH ME

It's possible to do exactly what we've set out in this book— to read the words carefully as part of a book within the Bible as a whole, to be sensitive to the vibe of the writing, to think about the local and historical context, to get a pretty accurate "read" on what the writer is saying—yet end up missing the point completely. Because while all these steps are really important, they aren't the main game. The purpose of reading the Bible is ultimately to hear God speak to us. We need to make sure we push through to this final stage. The most important question we can ask ourselves after reading the Bible is "What is God saying to me through this?" I'd even go so far as to say that if we can't answer that question, then we haven't read the text properly.

This doesn't come naturally to some of us. We like "doing things by numbers". We like processes and routine and reliable methods. We like coming up with the right answers. We enjoy working out how a particular part of the Bible points to Jesus. And all that's really good. We just have to be careful to remember that the goal of reading the Bible is *relational*. Working out what the text said "then" (in its original context to its original readers) is vital; but we spend time doing that not for its own sake, but so that we can hear what God is saying to his people *right now*. We have to work out how the text *applies to us*. For many people (including me) that's the hard bit.

As we'll see in a moment, it is possible to expect the *wrong* things from reading the Bible. But it's also possible *not to expect enough*: rather than approaching the Bible as an opportunity to listen to the God who loves us, we treat it like a textbook to be mastered, supplying important information.

When we slip into reading the Bible like this, any personal Bible study (or small group studies, or preaching in church) will tend to be very dull. We'll invest far too much time trying to nail down obscure details, and not enough time answering the question "What is God saying to me/ us today? What does this truth mean for me right now?" Let's make sure we don't make the trip back to the Bible's original context only to forget to come back home!

MISTAKE #2: MAKING THE BIBLE ALL ABOUT ME

The second mistake is exactly the opposite. Instead of getting too caught up in reading the Bible carefully and working out only what it meant *back then*, for some of us the danger is that we ditch all of that in our impatience to get to what God is saying to me (or us) *right now*.

There's something great about a longing to hear from God as he speaks right into the messy details of our world today. But the problem is that reading and understanding the Bible takes time. Unfortunately, there are no shortcuts available!

I have a weakness for shortcuts, whether attempting (unsuccessfully) to cut a corner on the under-13s cross-country course, to paint metal gates without priming them first, to move furniture that takes two people to carry it on my own... you get the picture. And it always ends badly (detention, having to strip off the newly applied but flaky paint, having to have the wall replastered). Trying to take shortcuts when reading the Bible is equally damaging.

What kind of shortcuts am I talking about? Basically, trying to move straight from the words on the page to "us" without worrying about the context or the author's intention. Here's what that might look like:

"God said that to them so he's saying it to me"

Say you happen to be reading Jeremiah 29 v 11 (my mother-in-law's favourite verse!): "'For I know the plans I have for you,' declares the LORD, 'plans to prosper you and not to harm you, plans to give you hope and a future'". These are amazing words. But tempting though it is, if we read them the night before a job interview, we shouldn't assume we're going to get the job! In this verse, God through Jeremiah is telling the Jewish exiles in Babylon not to panic because, eventually (after 70 years), he will bring them back home, and his grand plans for his people are still going to work out. In that sense, it's not really about us. But that doesn't mean that what God is saying to us isn't powerful or emotionally affecting. If anything, it's *more* arresting and reassuring to hear God say that whether we get the job or not (or in the Israelites' case, whether their country gets invaded or not), *he is in control and is building his kingdom for his glory!*

"This happened then, so it's going to happen now"

At several points in the Bible, some remarkable things happen: people are healed, the laws of nature are suspended and subverted, and dead people are even brought back to life.

But just because God did something at one point in history for one individual (generally at a key moment in his unfolding plan, such as during the exodus or Jesus' ministry), that doesn't mean he's going to act like that every time you or I would like him to! I've been to a lot of funerals over the years, but I've yet to see someone knock on the coffin and raise the dead person. Of course, God is all-powerful. He could do that (and I'm still secretly hoping that he will one day). But that isn't the same thing as saying that because it happened then, I can expect it to happen now.

The same principle applies to what God says about the beginnings of the church in the book of Acts. What God did in 1st-century Jerusalem may not be precisely what God does in 21st-century Brisbane or Birmingham or Bangkok. Does God speak to us through these episodes in Scripture? Yes, he most certainly does. But rather than promising a repeat performance of every event, he uses them to underline that the message of the gospel is powerful, and that we can expect him to use it to bring people to new, spiritual life in every conceivable situation.

"These words resonate with me—so that must be what God is saying to me"

Sometimes we can read the words of Bible through the lens of our own experience or mood in a way that doesn't actually fit with what the Bible is saying. For example, imagine I'm having a lousy day in the middle of a lousier week. I happen to come across the sentence "Be still and know that I am God" in Psalm 46 v 10. Because of how I'm feeling, I cling to this as a reminder to be calm and trust that whatever happens, God has it covered.

The problem is that while being calm is good, and God does have it covered, that's not what Psalm 46 v 10 is about. In the verse before, God has smashed and burned all the military hardware of those opposing him—and the words of verse 10 are addressed to those he has just overpowered. So what he's saying is *Shut up*, or *Stop fighting and face the fact that I am God*. It's a command to stop opposing God. Of course, there is comfort in that too, but not in quite the same way.

Psalm 46 isn't encouraging us to go into a darkened room and empty our minds in a search for inner tranquillity. It is an instruction to submit to God, admitting that we don't have the answers and should probably stop talking! When we do stop fighting against God, and we realise that he is fighting for us, and always wins, it is immensely reassuring—even calming. But the truth of this verse is bigger and richer than simply "calm down".

The thing about shortcuts is that they look so attractive. But when it comes to reading the Bible, they always end up in a dead end.

WHY THE BIBLE IS <u>FOR</u> ME (EVEN IF IT ISN'T <u>ABOUT</u> ME)

So what are we to do? The challenge is to remember that the Bible is FOR me, even though it isn't really ABOUT me.

That's basically what Paul says to Timothy in the verse that appeared at the start of this chapter: "All Scripture is God-breathed and is useful for teaching, rebuking, correcting and training in righteousness, so that the servant of God may be thoroughly equipped for every good work". As God speaks to us through the Bible, he teaches us, puts us straight on things and trains us to live like him. He constantly reminds us of what he has done for us and will do for us in the Lord Jesus. It's not about us, but it is for us. Three basic principles will help us not to lose sight of this.

PRINCIPLE #1: THE MAIN THING IN THE TEXT IS THE MAIN THING GOD IS SAYING TO US

This may actually be the most important point in this entire book! Remembering this simple principle will keep us on the straight and narrow whatever we are reading in the Bible: the main thing in the text is *always* the main thing God is saying to us.

The story of Daniel in the lions' den (in Daniel 6) is a beautiful illustration of this. It's a brilliantly narrated account of a senior government adviser being targeted by ambitious younger colleagues in the Babylonian court. Because of Daniel's complete integrity (6 v 4-5), they realise the only way they can get him into trouble is through his commitment to God—which they do. They trick the king into introducing a law against praying to anyone other than the king. Predictably, Daniel breaks the law by praying to the Lord and is sentenced to death. Daniel spends a night in the lions' den, from which he miraculously emerges unharmed.

The punchline of the story is spoken by Daniel's boss, King Darius, who says:

> People must fear and reverence the God of Daniel. For he is the living God and he endures for ever; his kingdom will not be destroyed, his dominion will never end. He rescues and he saves; he performs signs and wonders in the heavens and on the earth. He has rescued Daniel from the power of the lions.
> (Daniel 6 v 26-27)

It's not subtle. The main thing about the story isn't anything to do with Daniel—it's about Daniel's God. As in the rest of the book of Daniel, the point is that God is the sovereign God, who rules over kings and empires, hungry lions and sneaky civil servants, and who rescues his people. That's the main thing that God has to say to us in this part of the Bible. Which brings us to the second principle.

PRINCIPLE #2: THE MESSAGE OF THE TEXT MAY PLAY OUT DIFFERENTLY IN OUR CONTEXT

Daniel 6 makes it very clear that God is in charge, and that he can be trusted. For Daniel, that meant he was rescued from the ravenous beasts and lived to fight another day. But what about for us? Is the message that God will protect us from all danger and ensure we never suffer harm? Not necessarily.

Earlier in the book of Daniel (in chapter 3), three of Daniel's friends got into terrible trouble for refusing to bow down before a giant statue of their employer, an earlier king of Babylon called Nebuchadnezzar. Nebuchadnezzar was so enraged that he ordered that the three men be incinerated. Here's what they said:

> King Nebuchadnezzar, we do not need to defend ourselves before you in this matter. If we are thrown into the blazing furnace, the God we serve is able to deliver us from it, and he will deliver us from Your Majesty's hand. *But even if he does not, we want you to know, Your Majesty, that we will not serve your gods or worship the image of gold you have set up.*
>
> (Daniel 3 v 16-17, emphasis added)

Daniel's friends were completely convinced that God was in charge of all things. They knew he could get them out of the mess they were in. But they also knew that he may choose not to—and they wanted to make clear to Nebuchadnezzar that even if he didn't, it wouldn't change anything! As it happens, God rescued them too. But there are plenty of other people in the Bible who didn't get rescued—like the early Christian martyr Stephen, for example, who was stoned to death (Acts 6 – 7). The point is that God is in control, and that doesn't change, even if we're not rescued like Daniel and his friends.

The message of the text may be that God is the great healer, but that doesn't mean that we will be healed right now. The message of the text may be that God grants us an unshakeable peace—but he may give that to us in the midst of persecution and suffering. The message of the text may be that God will bring his enemies to judgment (something that Daniel got to see in his lifetime)—but we may well have to wait until Jesus' return for that to be worked out.

The message of the text may be plain, and it will always apply to us in some way—but we need to remember that the application may be different in our context.

PRINCIPLE #3: THE MESSAGE OF EVERY PART OF THE BIBLE IS "GOSPEL-SHAPED"

A good question to ask of every Bible passage we read is "How does this remind me of what Jesus has done for me?" If the whole Bible builds up to, explains, records and celebrates the coming of the Lord Jesus, then we can rest assured that every part of it is "gospel shaped". In other words, it announces what God has done for us in Christ rather than simply telling us to be good!

Of course, there is plenty in the Bible which encourages us to live God's way—but it always does this by telling us first what God has done (or, in the Old Testament, will do) for us to make this possible. If the main message we take from the text is something we have to do, we've probably gone wrong somewhere.

The main point of Daniel 6 isn't simply that we should pray more often (although that would be a great thing). Nor is it that God will rescue us from the "lions" in our life (although he might). The main point is that our God is the rescuing God. And when we view that truth through the lens of the gospel, we remember that it's Jesus who rescues us from sin and sets us free to enjoy life with him for ever. That's why we should read Daniel 6 and gasp in amazement, and thank God again for what he has done for us in the Lord Jesus.

And this truth will make a real difference to whatever we come up against this week, even if that probably won't involve lions. In the midst of deadlines, or family conflict, or mental-health issues, or in the face of hostility from our boss or peers or family because we are following Jesus, we can rest assured that our God can handle it—just as he could handle the lions. We can depend on him to give us the resources we need to keep going, and to work for the ultimate glory of Jesus, because he has already rescued us from sin and has promised to secure our future.

RICH... AND FRESH!

Reading the Bible carefully and thoughtfully may seem like hard work—but it is certainly worth it. Far from being an academic exercise, it allows us to hear all the richness of God's words to us. And incredibly, these ancient words speak into our lives with perpetual freshness. Reading the Bible isn't like watching a speech from the archives given by some politician 40 years ago. It's more like having the president or prime minister call you every day with a brief update on how things are going in the nation, and how you can help today! But even that doesn't do it justice— for the God who speaks is the God who made us and saved us and who loves us more than we can ever know or even imagine.

That's more than enough motivation to open the Bible today, ready to ask, "What is God saying to me right now through his word?"

YOUR TURN o -

Let's revisit the two passages we looked at in the exercise at the end of chapter 4, and work through the three principles described on pages 93-97.

Read Acts 12 v 1-24

1. *The main thing in the text is the main thing God is saying to us.* Look at your answer to question 4 on page 69. What is the main thing God is saying to us through this passage?

2. *The message of the text may play out differently in our context.* How did that main thing play out for the people in this passage? How might it play out for you?

3. *The message of every part of the Bible is "gospel shaped".* How does this remind you of what Jesus has done for you? How does it link to the gospel?

4. Looking at your answers to questions 1-3, what is God saying to you today? What does this truth mean for you right now?

Read Exodus 1 v 1-22 o -

1. *The main thing in the text is the main thing God is saying to us.* Look at your answer to question 4 on page 70. What is the main thing God is saying to us through this passage?

2. *The message of the text may play out differently in our context.* How did that main thing play out for the people in this passage? How might it play out for you?

3. *The message of every part of the Bible is "gospel shaped".* How does this remind you of what Jesus has done for you? How does it link to the gospel?

4. Looking at your answers to questions 1-3, what is God saying to you today? What does this truth mean for you right now?

7. OVER TO YOU

"I delight in your decrees;
I will not neglect your word."
(Psalm 119 v 16)

In the early part of this book, my great concern was to convince you of two astonishing truths: that the Bible is a remarkable book, breathed out by almighty God himself; and, even more astonishingly, that ordinary people like us can hear what he is saying by reading the words on the page in front of us. Although at one level, we need God to work in us through the Spirit to help us to get what a Bible passage is about (which he just *loves* to do), at another level, the key skill is simply that of reading—reading words, sentences and paragraphs. When we read carefully, the Bible is very clear, even though it is immensely rich (chapters 1 and 2).

We explored the richness of the Bible when we considered how to work out the vibe of a text (chapter 3). Not only has God spoken to us through all kinds of writers (whose personalities still somehow shine through, even though the words are also God's); he has done it in all kinds of ways. Different styles, tones and types of writing are all harnessed to produce different effects and reactions in us as we read, as God works through this book to make us more like Christ. That's why getting the "vibe" matters so much. In fact, it's one of the most important steps (along with reading what the text actually says, rather than what we think it says) in identifying the main thing(s) that God is saying to us through a passage (chapter 4).

To help us pick up the vibe and the main thing, we need to learn to read every part of the Bible in context—working out who it was written for, what was going on in the world at that moment, and how it fits into the grand sweep of God's masterplan to bring glory to the Lord Jesus (chapter 5). And once we've done all that, we're set up to ask the most significant question of all (chapter 6): *What is God saying to me right now through his word?*

I hope you've found it this approach useful as you've taken (or retaken!) your first steps in reading the Bible. But now it's time for a confession: if we want to read the Bible well, we actually need to do some of this in *reverse order*. When we're trying to get our heads around how the Bible works, it makes perfect sense to start with the words, and then "zoom out" towards the context. But when it comes to actually reading the Bible day after day, month after month, for the rest of our lives (which I pray that you'll do), it's best to start with what we've just looked at in chapter 5 (context) and jump back to the words (chapter 2). After that, we should focus on the vibe (chapter 3) and the meaning (chapter 4) before coming to application (chapter 6). But rather than leaving you to retrace your steps on your own, here is a six-step guide to reading the Bible which sums up everything you've read so far.

A 6-STEP GUIDE TO READING THE BIBLE

STEP #1: PRAY

The simplest and most sure-fire way to make sure that we don't read the Bible merely for interest but to hear God speak is to pray before we read it. It's also a healthy reminder that we do need God to enable us to get what he's saying to us, through the power of the Holy Spirit. Wonderfully, when we pray like this, God has promised that he will answer! (See Proverbs 2 v 1-6.)

STEP #2: CONTEXT

As we start to read, we need to get our bearings. Where are we in the Bible (especially in relation to the coming of Jesus)? What's going on in the world at this point? What are the "local factors" (if any) affecting this part of the Bible? (Note: One of the advantages of reading through the Bible passage by passage, book by book, is that the context only changes when we move to a new book. A more "random" approach to reading makes it much easier to completely lose our bearings.)

STEP #3: READ

The next step is simple but obviously vital—read the passage. Don't worry too much about trying to work out all the details at this stage; just read through the whole text you are looking at to familiarise yourself with what's actually there.

STEP #4: VIBE

As we start to read, we need to be sensitive to the vibe, asking ourselves questions like: Is this part of the Bible seeking to encourage or correct or shock or subvert or teach or warn? Is this a narrative? A direct prophetic message from God? A song or poem celebrating God's splendour and power? A quirky and provocative reflection on the messy details of life? A raw outpouring of sadness? You get the idea.

STEP #5: WORDS

Then it's time to get down to the nitty-gritty of what the words mean, and how they fit together. We'll need to work hard to pay attention to the words, the emphasis, the flow of the argument, and the allusions to other parts of the Bible. (This takes time, but it does get easier!) Now it's also time to work out the main thing the text is saying to its original audience.

STEP #6: APPLICATION

The first five steps set us up for this final one, which is applying the text to ourselves, our church and our world.

This is where we connect what God said "back then" to what God is saying to us today, in the light of the death and resurrection of the Lord Jesus. If we have understood the text properly, this application will always be "gospel-shaped" (driven by what God has done for us in Jesus, rather than simply telling us to do stuff).

So that's it. Six steps to reading the Bible in a way that will change our lives. What does that look like in practice?

TWO FINAL (HARD) EXAMPLES

Time for another confession. As you may have picked up, most of the examples I've used throughout this book have been drawn from narratives. The only problem with that is that for many of us, reading narrative comes fairly naturally. To put it bluntly, I've picked pretty easy examples to illustrate the principles. But what about the large sections of the Bible that aren't in story form? What about the poetry, and the prophecy, and everything else?

In my defence, in a short book like this there just isn't space to deal with every kind of writing in the Bible—not least because lots of parts of the Bible give their own unique twist on a common "style" (so the Gospels are a unique kind of biography, but each of them has a slightly different vibe and approach; Paul's letters work very differently to John's letters, and so on). But even so, this approach *really does* work with every part of the Bible—so we'll look at a couple of slightly harder examples to finish.

AN OLD TESTAMENT EXAMPLE:
LAMENTATIONS 3 v 22-27

[22] Because of the LORD's great love we are not
consumed,

    for his compassions never fail.

[23] They are new every morning;

    great is your faithfulness.

[24] I say to myself, "The LORD is my portion;

    therefore I will wait for him."

[25] The LORD is good to those whose hope is in him,

    to the one who seeks him;

[26] it is good to wait quietly

    for the salvation of the LORD.

[27] It is good for a man to bear the yoke

    while he is young. (Lamentations 3 v 22-27)

After praying (Step #1), we need to think about the context (Step #2) of Lamentations. In our English Bibles, Lamentations is helpfully paired with Jeremiah (who probably wrote it). Jeremiah was the prophet charged with speaking God's words to the kingdom of Judah just before, during and after the Babylonian invasion, when King Nebuchadnezzar's armies destroyed Jerusalem and anyone who was anyone was taken into exile in Babylon. This was a low point in the history of God's people. They desperately needed God to do something dramatic, but felt completely abandoned by him.

Having grasped that, we should then *read* through the text (Step #3). Which takes us to the vibe (Step #4).

The clue to the vibe of Lamentations is the name of the book! Almost everything in the book is pretty miserable. It was an intense time—and these are intense words. Lamentations is an "in the moment", unsanitised reaction to the unthinkable events of the exile. Almost the whole book is raw and extreme. In fact, Lamentations 3 v 22-27 contains just about the only upbeat statements there are. This section is a little shaft of light in the midst of otherwise unrelenting sadness and despair.

Step #5 is to look at the words themselves. This whole chapter of Lamentations (and in fact, the whole book) is very carefully and artfully put together. In chapter 3, each little three-lined section starts with successive letters of the Hebrew alphabet (some Bibles make that clear in the text, others add a footnote). There are 22 sections, with three verses in each, making 66 verses overall.

It's pretty clear that the main focus of these two sections (3 v 22-24 and 25-27) is God's faithfulness to his people, even when the pressure is on. They are not totally "consumed" because his commitment to them "never fails" (v 22). It is constantly being refreshed (v 23), which means they can count on him to come through on his commitment to them. The central assertion is simply "Great is your faithfulness" (v 23)!

For the first readers, this was an encouragement to hang in there when their world had just been smashed (literally and metaphorically) by the Babylonians: to trust in God even when life is falling apart. He is their "portion" (of land), even when their actual inheritance has been lost (v 24). It is God himself whom they need to learn to treasure—and the sooner in life they do that the better (v 27). The fact that this reassurance comes in the midst of a sea of misery, as the events surrounding the exile are described in vivid and dramatic terms, just further highlights the bullet-proof commitments that God gives to his people.

Now, we are clearly not in the same situation as the people of Judah in the 6th century BC (unless the Babylonians have been invading again). So how can we apply this passage (Step #6) responsibly to ourselves?

The key is, as always, to focus on the main thing—on the faithfulness of God. God is just as committed to us as he was to his people in Lamentations 3. But now we see God's faithfulness in a different, cross-shaped light. It is Jesus himself—in his incarnation, life, death and resurrection—who has put on display God's willingness to go to any lengths for our sake. Because of Jesus, we know, as Paul wrote, that even "if we are faithless, he remains faithful, for he cannot disown himself" (2 Timothy 2 v 13). Reading Lamentations 3 is a powerful reminder of the fact that even if our world is falling apart, we can still count on God, who has shown us his great love and given us himself in the Lord Jesus. Nothing can ever change that.

A NEW TESTAMENT EXAMPLE:
REVELATION 5 v 1-5

¹ Then I saw in the right hand of him who sat on the throne a scroll with writing on both sides and sealed with seven seals. ² And I saw a mighty angel proclaiming in a loud voice, "Who is worthy to break the seals and open the scroll?" ³ But no one in heaven or on earth or under the earth could open the scroll or even look inside it. ⁴ I wept and wept because no one was found who was worthy to open the scroll or look inside. ⁵ Then one of the elders said to me, "Do not weep! See, the Lion of the tribe of Judah, the Root of David, has triumphed. He is able to open the scroll and its seven seals." (Revelation 5 v 1-5)

Start by praying (Step #1), and then think about the context (Step #2) of Revelation. In the history of the church, people have argued more passionately about the meaning of the book of Revelation than just about any other! But remembering the context is the best way to make sure we're on firm ground. The quickest way to check the context is usually to glance at the opening verses (or chapters) of the book. If we do that, we see that this letter was written to churches who were under pressure (1 v 4 and chapters 2 – 3)—both from the Roman authorities and from other people who didn't like their message (including both Jewish people and pagan idol-worshippers). Over the years lots of people have tried to tie what's described in Revelation to particular moments in the history of the Roman Empire, but the jury's still out on that. In any case, it's clear that the Christians it addresses were living in difficult circumstances.

At this point, read the text (Step #3) and then think about the vibe (Step #4).

Admittedly, some parts of Revelation are pretty strange. There are symbolic multi-horned beasts crawling around, ear-splitting trumpet blasts, horsemen, dragons and more. There isn't really anything quite like it anywhere else in the Bible (apart from a chapter or two in the Old Testament prophets Ezekiel and Zechariah, and the book of Daniel). But that shouldn't come as a surprise. At the start of the book, John describes what he's writing in three ways: he addresses his readers as in a letter (1 v 4), but he calls it a "prophecy" (v 3, like the Old Testament prophetic writings) and an "apocalypse" or "revelation" (v 1, a book which explains the way things really are). In other words, this is a book like no other.

But like the New Testament letters and the Old Testament prophets, this explanation of reality is written to help God's people to keep going under pressure. It is weird and wacky, but its dramatic language and imagery are designed to help God's people to stay grounded and to trust in God's sovereignty, whatever happens. In other words, like Lamentations 3 (which is very different in style), the whole book, and our passage in particular, are written to reassure.

There is some very specific "local" background information which helps to make sense of this passage. If you were a Roman citizen, and you wrote your will, you summarised it on the back of the scroll, and then got seven people to witness it and then put their seals on the back. Those seals could only be broken after you had died, when a trustworthy executor was given the job of fulfilling the terms of the will. Nothing could happen until then. The scene in Revelation 5 shows something similar, except this "scroll" isn't a will. Instead, we're meant to be reminded of Daniel 12 v 1-4, in which a scroll—describing how God will build his kingdom and save his people—is sealed up "until the time of the end" (Daniel 12 v 4). This scroll is what John sees.

So what about Step #4, the words themselves? The trickiest thing about Revelation is that almost every sentence that John writes is packed with quotations and allusions to the Old Testament. That makes it hard for a new reader—but the more you read the rest of the Bible, the clearer Revelation becomes!

In the Bible, it is really only God who sits on a throne, so verse 1 is clearly talking about God the Father. And what's in his right hand? It's that document, with writing on both sides, sealed up with seven seals, describing key events in God's rescue plan which can't be rolled out until someone who is properly "qualified" shows up to open the scroll. The problem is that no one is "worthy" to open the scroll and bring about the rescue it describes (v 2-3). So

John weeps uncontrollably at this desperately sad news (v 4). Until, that is, his heavenly guide reminds him that Jesus' great victory (his death and resurrection) means that he is qualified to open the scroll (v 5). Jesus is called the "Lion of the tribe of Judah" (an allusion to Genesis 49 v 9) and "the Root of David" (an idea found in Isaiah 11 v 1-10). The point of both phrases is to underline that Jesus Christ is the one promised by God in whom all his plans are brought to reality.

So what does this have to say to us (Step #6)? It is a reminder that because Jesus has come, the outcome of history is certain. God will build his church. His grip on us is sure, and we are utterly secure in him. So whether we are being persecuted by the government, or mocked by our friends, or marginalised by our neighbours, we can be sure that God is on his throne, directing history itself for our good and the glory of Jesus.

NOW READ ON... AND ON

Hopefully, reading this book has convinced you that reading the Bible isn't as hard as you thought. Yes, it's from a different "world". Yes, it's different from any other book. But in God's kindness, he has set things up so that when we read it, we hear his voice, speaking right into our world, right now, by the power of his Spirit. And incredibly, through this book, God speaks to every believer—including you—no matter how long you've been a Christian or how little or much you know. You can hear him just as clearly as someone who's been reading the Scriptures for decades! The Bible is God's precious gift to you.

So what do we do now? We read on. And on. And on. And we do so knowing that because God himself speaks to us through his word, we will never get past our need to read this book, and to listen to our God. As the 19th-century English preacher Charles Spurgeon once said, "Nobody ever outgrows Scripture; the book widens and deepens with our years". May that be your experience, as you take this book, read it, and hear the very voice of God.

YOUR TURN o -

Choose any passage of the Bible and work through the six steps. Jot down notes as you go. If you don't know which to choose, try Luke 8 v 40-56.

1. Pray

2. Context

3. Read

4. Vibe

5. Words

6. Application

APPENDIX:
WHAT IS THE BIBLE?

The Bible is unlike every other book that any of us will pick up. Even the fact that many editions of the Bible are printed in tiny letters in double columns on remarkably thin paper can be a little disconcerting. And that's before we even think about reading it. So, if you're relatively new to the Bible and aren't really sure what's in there or where it came from, here are some useful things to know before reading the rest of the book.

1. THE BIBLE ISN'T JUST ONE BOOK

For a start, the Bible, strictly speaking, isn't one book but a collection of 66 books within the same cover (the word Bible actually comes from the Greek word for "books" or "scrolls"). These books emerged periodically over the course of the history of the nation of Israel, from around 1400 BC to the 1st century AD. The longest books are over 30,000 words long—the shortest have fewer than 300 words! Some of them were written by individuals, some were team efforts, and some are completely anonymous.

In our English Bibles, the books have all come to bear standard names. Some of the books bear the names of the writers (like the prophet Amos, or the letters of 1 and 2 Peter) or the main character (like Joshua). Other books are letters to particular churches or individuals which are known by their recipient(s) (so Ephesians was written to the church in Ephesus, and Titus was written to a guy called Titus!). Still other books go by titles they were given in Greek in around the third century BC. This is where Genesis—the "book of beginnings"—and Exodus—the "exit"—get their names.

2. THE BIBLE IS A BOOK OF TWO HALVES

Even though the Bible is one large collection, it is also divided into two "halves". The first section is longer and older, and is called the "Old Testament"; the second is shorter and later, and goes by the name of the "New Testament". The word "testament" means a "sworn statement", so both parts of the Bible are making a claim about something important. For Christians, the Bible's claims are all about the Lord Jesus Christ—the Old Testament speaks of our need of him and the New Testament is about what he has done, is doing and will do for us.

The Old Testament is written almost entirely in ancient Hebrew. We aren't entirely sure how the books of the Old Testament were collected, or who decided what to include or not to include. But certainly by the time of Jesus in the 1st century AD, it had long been accepted that there were 24 books in the "canon" (approved collection) of the Old Testament. These 24 books correspond to the 39 in English Bibles today (in the Hebrew edition, the six books of Samuel, Kings and Chronicles are all counted as one book, as are the twelve "Minor" Prophets). The books were generally arranged in three sections: the Law (the first five books), the Prophets (divided into the historical books of Joshua, Judges, Samuel and Kings, and then the Prophets "proper", like Isaiah and Jeremiah), and the Writings (everything else, including the Psalms). Sometimes the internal order of the Writings varied, but everything else was "fixed" in ancient times.

When it comes to the New Testament, things are a little clearer. All the books were written in everyday Greek (Greek was the common language of the otherwise multilingual region at that time), and they were all written within around 60 years of Jesus' death. Four "Gospels" set out the events of Jesus of Nazareth's life, birth, death and resurrection, and explain their significance; the book of Acts tells us what happened in the immediate aftermath of the resurrection; and the rest of the New Testament books (mostly letters) were written to help the emerging Christian movement work out how to live in the light of Jesus' message.

How were these books selected to be included in the Bible? Even in the New Testament itself, it's clear that the authority of teaching (and writing) was dependent on the authority of the writer. If the writer was an eye witness to Jesus' life and work (one of those "apostles" handpicked by Jesus to lead his church) or closely associated with the apostles, then the book could lay claim to authority. Matthew and John were apostles, and their Gospels were written from first-hand experience. Mark was a close associate of the apostle Peter, and Luke of the apostle Paul. All the other New Testament books have a similar link to Jesus' inner circle. Books were included on the "approved list" (or canon) on this basis, as well as on the evidence of their authenticity (were they actually written by the person whose name was attached to them?) and their usefulness to a wide range of churches. At points there was some discussion about whether or not particular books should be on the list (notably the book of James, written by one of Jesus' half-brothers), but it seems that very quickly—and certainly by the end of the 2nd century— the list of New Testament books was as stable as that of the Old Testament.

Given that the Bible was written over hundreds of years, in several different languages, in multiple different nations for many different purposes, the most remarkable thing about it is the way that despite the variety, the whole collection "hangs together" and presents a unified message. For Christians, this is because God himself stands behind the Bible as its ultimate author.

3. THE BIBLE HASN'T CHANGED OVER TIME

Given how long ago they were written, it's no surprise that the original scrolls on which the Bible writers wrote no longer exist. This is entirely normal for ancient manuscripts. But the original manuscripts were copied, and those copies were copied, and those copies were copied, down the generations, until we arrive at the manuscripts we rely on today. Some people worry that this means we can't be sure that what we have now is the same as what was originally written. But we can be confident that the text of the Bible hasn't changed because of the staggering number and quality of copies available.

For instance, we now have about 5,500 different Greek manuscripts containing at least parts of the New Testament. Those manuscripts date from just a few decades after the New Testament was written through to about 400 years later. That's a lot of copies! And that isn't counting the tens of thousands of early translations into other ancient languages, and the hundreds of thousands of quotations of the text in early Christian writings. The fact that the multiple copies of the biblical text have so few discrepancies between them means that we can be certain that we have an accurate record of what the text of the Bible actually said.

Compare that with something like Julius Caesar's great work Caesar's Gallic Wars. It was written sometime in the 1st century BC. The earliest copies we have were made over a thousand years later—and we only have ten. Yet nobody really doubts that what we have in that ancient book is what Caesar wrote. So we have even more reason to be confident that what we have in the Bible is what the authors originally wrote.

4. THE BIBLE NOW HAS AN INTERNAL REFERENCING SYSTEM

One of the things you will notice when you open a Bible is that unlike most other books, the text is littered with numbers—generally of two sizes. The large numbers divide the text into "chapters", and the smaller ones divide each chapter into "verses". Most English Bibles also add paragraph headings, which attempt to summarise the point of each block of text. But it's important to remember that these numbers and headings were not always part of the Bible.

Originally, the text was written in unpunctuated, continuous script—usually on scrolls or sheets of parchment or vellum (animal skin)—with slightly larger spaces to mark breaks in thought or syntax. As time went on, Jewish scribes adopted all kinds of small text marks to indicate where these breaks occurred in the Hebrew Bible. By the 4th or 5th century AD, numbers started appearing in some Greek manuscripts—a practice followed by some of the monks who devoted vast amounts of time and energy to copying ancient manuscripts (often using intricate and beautifully crafted script). By the 12th century, as early universities got going, biblical scholars and teachers started to devise their own systems (like the brilliantly named "Peter the Chanter", who died in 1197). The chapter divisions we use today were (probably) the work of a man called Stephen Langton (c.1150-1228), an Englishman who studied and taught in Paris, before returning home to become Archbishop of Canterbury.

Several hundred years later, after the printing press had burst on the scene, a Frenchman called Robert Estienne was responsible for dividing chapters into smaller units (called verses). His divisions were used in the publication of the English "Geneva Bible" of 1560, and since then basically every printed Bible has followed this scheme. It wasn't long before publishers started adding paragraph headings (generally helpful, but not always entirely accurate), footnotes and all sorts of other "clutter"! Much of this is useful, but just remember that the words on the page are the only thing that's original.

5. TRANSLATING THE BIBLE IS A BIT MORE COMPLICATED THAN WE MIGHT THINK

If you have ever tried to buy a Bible, you have probably discovered that it isn't quite as straightforward as you might think. It turns out that there is a rather a lot of choice. They are packaged for men, women, teenagers, kids and every other conceivable demographic. They come with space to write, added prayers and various wisdom from down through the ages. Some are printed in two columns on ridiculously thin paper edged with gold leaf, and others come in camouflage colours ready for use in all weathers.

But slightly more confusingly than the marketing, you can actually buy Bibles which have different words on the page, taking your pick from those which are contemporary, international, or standard, or even come with royal approval. So why is that?

The fact that there are all kinds of translations of the Bible isn't a product of Christians' failure to agree—it's just a consequence of the challenges of translating an ancient book into the language people speak today. Any translator has to make a basic choice: do I try to stick as closely as possible to the words and rhythms of the writer or do I try to capture the heart of what they're saying and express it as naturally as possible in the target language?

An example may help. Where I am from in Ireland, the word "craic" (pronounced "crack") doesn't describe an illegal substance but a particular quality of social experience—as in "Last night was great craic!" If I had to "translate" that phrase, I could just say, "Last night was great fun", but that leaves something to be desired. Or I could say, "Last night, there was a richness to our time together and we laughed a lot", which is more accurate but is much longer than the original (and something no self-respecting Irish person would actually say). Or I could say, "We had a brilliant time last night", which captures the essence but has completely changed the shape of the sentence. Notice how all three versions capture the basic meaning. It's just that they have particular strengths and weaknesses. That's why translating is hard work! It's also why there will always be a place for new translations.

The fact that the Bible itself was written in a down-to-earth style for ordinary people means that it is important to make sure that everyone today has the chance to read its words in their own language too. And if that's to happen, it means the Bible needs to be translated into every language, and into language that people actually use and understand. (Which, incidentally, is why the King James or Authorised Version of the Bible, brilliant piece of work though it is, probably shouldn't be the version you choose—unless your mother tongue is Elizabethan English!)

Translations that focus more on expressing ideas naturally in contemporary language tend to be the easiest to read. Those that try to stick more closely to the patterns of the original can be great for studying the text carefully, but they can sound clumsy and slightly odd. So, it really does depend on what you are looking for. The good news is that today we have some great choices of careful, thoughtful and faithful translations of the text into contemporary English. If you'd like a suggestion, I'd start with the Christian Standard Bible or the New International Version.

Do remember, though, that no translation is perfect. My favourite example of that is the so-called "Wicked Bible" of 1631, which gained infamy because it left out a word (accidentally!) and so told people: "Do commit adultery". Even the best translations have weaknesses and tend to date over time as language itself shifts.

The fact that faithful translations can sound quite different doesn't need to send us into a tailspin. Good translations will always convey the same basic message. And the great news is that the same God who stood behind the production of the original continues to work through his words (even in translation) to bring about real-time change in the lives of people like us.

6. GOD SPEAKS THROUGH THE BIBLE

So what is the Bible? The Bible is a collection of books, gathered into two main sections, the Old and the New Testaments, which point forward to Jesus and then explain the significance of his life, death and resurrection. The books in the Bible were selected carefully and very early on. The text of the Bible as we have it is what the original authors wrote. The numbers and headings are useful added tools. And the English translations of the Bible are very reliable.

That really only leaves one more thing to say. It's actually the reason behind this book. *By the power of the Holy Spirit, God speaks through the words of the Bible.* Or, to turn that sentence around, *when we read the Bible, we hear God's voice.* Not in some spooky sense but in a very real, down-to-earth, normal way. The words and sentences we read were written for us and address us. As we read, God speaks.

That's why learning to read the Bible properly matters. That's why I've written this book.

RECOMMENDED
RESOURCES

The aim of this book has been to help you to see that you can read the Bible yourself! But sometimes we all need a little help.

If, as you read the Bible, you have a specific question, the best resource you have available is the other people in your church. Friends who have been reading the Bible for a little longer than you would no doubt love to chat about your question—and asking it will probably help them to think in a new way about the Bible, too. You could also try Ligonier Ministries "Ask Ligonier" chat feature, which will point you in the direction of solid answers: https://ask.ligonier.org/.

For help with the context of Bible passages, a good study Bible can be valuable. These tend to have introductions to each book of the Bible (with information on the author, when it was written, why it was written, key themes and overview) as well as notes that explain some of the "local context" details. The CSB Study Bible, the NIV

Zondervan Study Bible or the ESV Study Bible would be a good place to start.

To help you get into a habit of reading the Bible every day, try *Explore* Bible-reading notes. Each day there's a passage to read and questions to answer which follow the same kind of steps as we've covered in this book. The notes also provide some helpful context.

If you've got more questions about the reliability of the Bible, try *Can I Really Trust the Bible?* by Barry Cooper (The Good Book Company, 2014) or *Can We Trust the Gospels?* by Peter J. Williams (Crossway, 2018).

And finally, if you've enjoyed this book and are looking for a similar introduction to all the other parts of the Christian life beyond reading the Bible, then I've written a book for that too! It's called *Need to Know: Your Guide to the Christian Life* (The Good Book Company, 2020).

thegoodbook
COMPANY

BIBLICAL | RELEVANT | ACCESSIBLE

At The Good Book Company, we are dedicated to helping Christians and local churches grow. We believe that God's growth process always starts with hearing clearly what he has said to us through his timeless word—the Bible.

Ever since we opened our doors in 1991, we have been striving to produce Bible-based resources that bring glory to God. We have grown to become an international provider of user-friendly resources to the Christian community, with believers of all backgrounds and denominations using our books, Bible studies, devotionals, evangelistic resources, and DVD-based courses.

We want to equip ordinary Christians to live for Christ day by day, and churches to grow in their knowledge of God, their love for one another, and the effectiveness of their outreach.

Call us for a discussion of your needs or visit one of our local websites for more information on the resources and services we provide.

Your friends at The Good Book Company

thegoodbook.com | thegoodbook.co.uk
thegoodbook.com.au | thegoodbook.co.nz
thegoodbook.co.in